Table of Contents

D1540660

Personal and Imaginative Writing

Functional Communication

Nonfiction/Reporting

Opinion Making

Virginia DeBolt: *Write! Cooperative Learning and the Writing Process*
Kagan Cooperative Learning. • 1 (800) WEE CO-OP

I

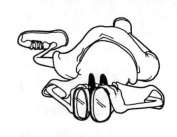

the Structures

Where to Find

Virginia DeBolt: *Write! Cooperative Learning and the Writing Process*
Kagan Cooperative Learning • 1 (800) WEE CO-OP

II

Write!

Cooperative Learning & The Writing Process

Virginia DeBolt

In consultation with Dr. Spencer Kagan

Kagan

COOPERATIVE LEARNING

Kagan Cooperative Learning
27134 Paseo Espada, Suite 302
San Juan Capistrano, CA 92675

ISBN: 1-879097-20-6

the Structures

	Basic Description	See Also
Pairs Edit	44	178
Pairs Experiment	44	96
Pairs Rehearse	45	178
Partners	45	127
Poetry Reading	46	80
Rallytable	46	189
Read In	46	58, 162
Roam the Room	46	116, 138, 166
Rotating Feedback	47	126, 172
Roundrobin	47	116, 155, 166, 172
Roundtable	47	74, 80, 90, 116, 133, 134, 154, 172
Roundtable Word Web	47	125
Simultaneous Roundtable	48	80, 120
Spend-A-Buck	48	91
Story Problem Planners	48	57
Team Brainstorm	48	119
Team Collaboration	49	73, 154
Team Confer	49	74, 162
Team Discussion	49	73, 80, 91, 96, 100, 120, 125, 154
Team Interview	49	58, 139, 161
Team Performance	50	74
Team Poem	50	80
Team Posters	50	120
Team Rehearsal	50	74
Teams Consult	50	126, 171
Think-Pair-Share	50	165
Think-Pair-Square	52	90
Think-Write-Pair-Compare	52	100, 181
Think-Write-Pair-Share	52	134, 177, 183
Word Webbing	52	56
Write-What-I-Act	53	115, 133

Virginia DeBolt: *Write! Cooperative Learning and the Writing Process*
Kagan Cooperative Learning • 1 (800) WEE CO-OP

III

the Writing Process

Structures &

IV

Virginia DeBolt: *Write! Cooperative Learning and the Writing Process*
Kagan Cooperative Learning • 1 (800) WEE CO-OP

Structures &
the Writing Process

Virginia DeBolt: *Write! Cooperative Learning and the Writing Process*
Kagan Cooperative Learning Co. • 1 (800) WEE CO-OP

V

Structures &

VI

Virginia DeBolt: *Write! Cooperative Learning and the Writing Process*
Kagan Cooperative Learning • 1 (800) WEE CO-OP

Foreword

by Dr. Spencer Kagan

Cooperative learning and writing — it's a natural marriage. Those of us who use cooperative learning structures at various stages in the writing process can't imagine fostering writing fully without cooperative learning at each stage. Perform a simple experiment: Let students in teams talk about anything, and then have them write about it. Not only are they more motivated to write, they show among other things greater fluency, richer vocabulary, superior perspective, and better organization. Or perform a second experiment: After students have written a first draft, let them read it to a partner and discuss the ideas behind the writing before they rewrite. Again (even if the partner says little or nothing!), we observe a tremendous difference in the quality of the second draft, simply because students have heard themselves as they shared their writing with an audience.

Cooperative learning is a communicative process. And so, too, is writing. One process supports the other. Through cooperative learning we learn to trust and develop our own ideas and points of view, receive peer support, and see the world through the eyes of others. As we interact over the content of our writing we discover what we wish to express. Only when we feel safe — really safe — can we fully express what is in us to say. Cooperative learning provides a safe, interactive context which fosters fuller expression.

Virginia DeBolt's book is a valuable tool for any teacher fostering writing skills. For teachers who know the writing process well, there are many new suggestions and teaching aids to enrich the process. Not only does the book show how to get more from each stage of the writing process through cooperative learning, it provides numerous easy-to-implement, hands-on activities. For teachers who know cooperative learning structures well, there are many suggestions to expand the writing curriculum. And, there are several new twists on the structural approach — original structures, like Numbered Heads Apart, particularly suited to the writing process.

The book is different in several important ways from previous curriculum-specific books published by Kagan Cooperative Learning. As I read the book, I am reminded of the early vision behind our company, which was originally named "Resources for Teachers." My first book sprang from my desire to provide teachers with a variety of resources they would find useful. As we flip through the pages of Virginia's book we are struck with the range and power of the resources she has gathered to share. Flip the book open and land on a frame designed to provide success at an early stage of poetry writing; flip to another page and land on a die students roll to generate ideas; on another page we find an "Author's Award," ready to duplicate. The list of resources is long, including addresses for students to write, cards to make Formations come alive, Value Line strips, blackline of Proofreader's Marks, Peer Response Forms, Gambit Sheets, and blacklines so each student can record Writing Topics, Titles of Finished Writing, and Writing Skills which have been mastered. Virginia has found many things which work well to foster all types of writing. Her book springs from the instincts of a true teacher: She wants to share the knowledge she has gathered.

Write! divides writing into four main types: Personal/Imaginative; Functional Communication; Nonfiction/Reporting; and Opinion Making. Each type is subdivided, resulting in 18 styles of writing, ranging from Fiction to Persuasive Paragraphs. For each type of writing Virginia has written a chapter which contains lesson ideas, forms and blacklines, samples of student writing, use-

ful resources, philosophy, and suggestions. Virginia is eclectic and generous. If she has found a tool or a gem, she shares it — whether it a way to bind a book, or a bit of wisdom such as "We learn more from output than input." Her eclectic and generous nature has led Virginia to create a book you will not finish. You will find yourself coming back to *Write!* time and again for ideas, inspiration, resources, and tools.

Write! is not just eighteen lessons. Nay, it is a giant salad bar. For each type of writing, there is a basic lesson frame, and then Virginia has included a range of "Alternative Activities." As you use the book, you will discover that for each of the 18 types of writing, Virginia has provided ingredients and philosophy which are powerful resources to use as you prepare learning experiences adapted to the needs of your students.

Dr. Spencer Kagan

Virginia DeBolt: *Write! Cooperative Learning and the Writing Process*
Kagan Cooperative Learning • 1 (800) WEE CO-OP

2

Letter from the Author

Dear Educator,

One of my favorite joking remarks is, "I've spent over half my life locked up in a room filled with 30 ten-year-olds." During my years of teaching I have, however, ventured out of my room long enough to notice a few realities about education. One of those realities is that children don't do much writing in school. They use up a great deal of paper, wear down a great many pencils, and complete mountains of dittos, but they don't "write." Some research indicates that as little as 2% of a student's time is spent writing — and some of that is merely filling in sentence fragments on a worksheet.

Several summers ago, I ventured out of my classroom all the way to California to attend one of Spencer Kagan's workshops. Suddenly, I found myself doing a better job with kids than I had ever done before. Students became excited about learning, their faces lit up with expressions of dawning light that teachers often consider teaching's greatest reward. As a teacher and a writer, I had made a connection, completed a circuit, in cooperative learning. The idealistic quotation from Gibran's *The Prophet* that I propped on my desk the first year I taught seemed possible: "The teacher...(i)f he is indeed wise...does not bid you enter the house of his wisdom, but rather leads you to the threshold of your own mind."

If we accept the basic premise that children learn to write by writing, then we must allow them to do it. But quiet writing is not enough. There must be interaction, exchange, talk, response and discussion about writing going on in the classroom. That kind of active and interactive talk underpins the cooperative learning classroom.

Think again about the realities of education. Teachers are handed an English or Language Arts book and told that they will be held accountable for "covering the curriculum." That word — accountable — more and more has come to mean that the curriculum is test-driven; that teachers teach to the test. Looking through the English textbook, the teacher finds a scope and sequence chart listing writing skills such as letters, descriptive paragraphs, and book reports in the writing strand. However, close examination of the lessons often reveals that they are worksheet-based, not writing-based. **The evidence shows that teaching isolated language mechanics skills separately from actual writing does not lead to mastery or to learning that transfers from one writing situation to another.** That conflict led to the creation of this book.

Virginia DeBolt: *Write! Cooperative Learning and the Writing Process*
Kagan Cooperative Learning • 1 (800) WEE CO-OP

3

I have two goals in *Write! Cooperative Learning and the Writing Process.* One is to help you, the teacher, step away from textbook-driven lessons to have students do more "writing." Two, to use the Structural Approach to Cooperative Learning to accomplish this. To achieve these goals is to empower and to free both students and teachers.

Student Empowerment. Student empowerment comes through learning to use pair, team, and group writing conferences. When children learn to speak with each other in literate conversation about writing, they gain powerful lifelong learning potential as writers.

The child's participation as writer or helper in a writing conference signifies that writing is regarded as a process of refinement, something which has meaning for an audience, and allows the writer's voice to be heard. Students are empowered to become lifelong writers, capable of using writing to inform, to discover, to create, to share, to help, to convince, to relive. Writers become. Students become writers when they have many opportunities to write.

Teacher Empowerment. These lessons empower and free you by providing a structure which allows movement away from the nonwriting of the traditional workbook based curriculum. Use each lesson not just once, but again and again. Don't have students write just one poem, one editorial, one report. Feel free to adapt or to move the cooperative learning structures from one lesson to another. As an author who believes in the value of feedback, I welcome comments from teachers who use this book. I also welcome writing samples from students who complete these lessons.

Samples of children's writing are included with each lesson. They are unedited and uncorrected, except by the students. None of their spelling, capitalization or punctuation has been changed. You will notice that the range of "Samplings" is limited. Therefore I encourage and welcome samples of students' work from all grade levels using this book. In Appendix A at the end of the book, you will find a release form. Please include it with any work you send me so that students will receive proper credit if their work is published in future editions of this book. Mail them to Virginia DeBolt, c/o Kagan Cooperative Learning, 27134 Paseo Espada, Suite 302, San Juan Capistrano, CA 92675. Keep those cards and letters coming, folks.

Kagan's Work. Spencer Kagan's book, *Cooperative Learning,* published by Kagan Cooperative Learning, is the basic book for the Structural Approach to Cooperative Learning. Any reader unfamiliar with Kagan's work and book will find that it is the complete source of information on team formation, class management, theory, structures, and lesson design. The lessons described here are usable and understandable by teachers from any background. However, if you have not studied his book or attended his workshops, I urge that you do so.

This book consists of cooperative learning lesson designs. It can be used either to replace or supplement Language Arts textbook-based writing instruction. It is a bridge leading teachers and young writers away from textbook-based writing toward writing as a process. The lessons included may bear the same titles as the lessons on the scope and sequence charts of the English basals, but are designed to produce real writing, not worksheet writing.

Each lesson includes a page intended for use as a rough draft. Down the left side of each rough draft reproducible is a rectangular box labeled Peer Response. At the bottom of the box two gambits are included. These gambits are suggested as possible positive beginnings for comments by peers who critique the work. I suggest that you work with your students to develop more positive gambits before they enter into peer conferences for EVERY lesson. I can't stress strongly enough the importance of learning positive ways to deliver suggestions to budding writers.

You will find a description of the writing process in Chapter 3. Techniques and methods for assessment and evaluation of writing are examined in Chapter 4. The structures used in the lessons are fully described in Chapter 5. Teachers already familiar with Spencer Kagan's work on the Structural Approach will find several new structures aimed at the writing process. The main body of the book contains lesson designs. Sprinkled throughout the book are reproducible materials to aid you in using both the structures and the lessons. Following the last lesson is a chapter containing brief suggestions for responding to literature, and a chapter listing options in publishing children's work. Good writing!

Sincerely,

Virginia DeBolt

Virginia DeBolt
New Mexico, 1994

References

Gibran, Kahlil. *The Prophet.* New York: Alfred A. Knopf, 1963.

Kagan, Spencer. *Cooperative Learning.* San Juan Capistrano, CA: Kagan Cooperative Learning, 1993.

The Writing Process
—and—
Cooperative Learning

The writing process is cyclical. Around a hub of rewriting, revision, and conferring revolve prewriting, writing, proofreading, editing, and publishing like spokes of a wheel. See illustration on page 13.

Prewriting
Before writing, writers plan, visualize, predict, and incubate. A writer might daydream, think, talk, draw, chart, outline, make notes, create word webs, or jot down important phrases and words. Although these activities are defined as prewriting, writers may revert to the incubation stage at any time during writing. In the setting of a cooperative learning classroom, prewriting activities include work by individuals, pairs, teams, and the whole class. Many cooperative learning structures are suited to prewriting, including Corners, Folded Value Line, Formations, Round-robin, Team Interview, Brainstorming, Team Discussion, Think-Pair-Share, and Inside-Outside Circle. Prewriting activities will be more successful if concrete

experiences are provided involving the whole child in seeing, touching, and smelling. If you're writing a poem about a tree, go outside and have a tree experience. If you're writing a report on lady bugs, go outside and chase some in the clover. Want to do a lesson on writing directions? Bring in some Graham crackers, Hershey bars and marshmallows and make S'mores. Then have kids write those directions. Get real; get the kids involved. Use structures such as Think-Pair-Share, Inside-Outside Circle, Team Brainstorming, or Write-What-I-Act to generate language, vocabulary, concepts, and ideas.

With older children who are more comfortable with abstractions, guided imagery and visualization (an Imagine-Pair-Share or Imagine-Write-Pair-Share) will set the prewriting scene. The BLM Project Wild materials have some nice guided imagery experiences or you can just make up your own:

It's St. Patrick's Day and you are tiny as a toadstool. Approaching through the grass, you spy a leprechaun. Take a look at him. How is he dressed? What does he say?...

- **4-S Brainstorming**
- **Formations**
- **Inside-Outside Circle**
- **Roundrobin**
- **Team Discussion**
- **Team Interview**
- **Think-Pair-Share**

Prewriting Structures

Books and stories read aloud by the teacher are another form of prewriting. Stop reading in mid-chapter or mid-dialog and tell the students, "Write what comes next."

Professional writers advise neophyte writers to "write what you know." Experience, concepts, and language naming the concepts need to be built up by the teacher during prewriting so that the students "know" and, therefore, can write. Building a language and concept base while prewriting can require half (or more) of the total lesson time.

Writing

During the writing stage, writers strive to record the content of their ideas. Some writers, especially children, write quickly without paying much attention to the clarity of their thinking. Until we teach them otherwise, children often consider this first dash at a piece of writing to be the finished product. Effective writers return to their first draft to consider improvement and clarification.

Conferring/Rewriting

Conferring about content, rewriting, and revising the first draft — or the second or the third draft — are at the core of the writing process. Opal Wheeler, a journalist and teacher at Otero Junior College in Colorado, taught me, "The best stories are not written — they're rewritten." After Opal passed away, the college named a new library in her honor. Her picture hangs in the hall. Somewhere, perhaps carved in the stone above her portrait, it should say, "The best stories are not written — they're rewritten." Her message is still true. Share her dictum with young writers today and you give them a powerful key. It's the key to the door of effective written communication. Thanks, Opal.

Designed into Cooperative Learning are powerful structures for the accomplishment of the core activity of writing: conferring and rewriting. Students have opportunities for reaction and response to their writing. The free play of ideas and the opportunity to exchange thoughts is crucial in helping children view writing as a process rather than a product. Peers emerge as an interactive audience whose questions, concerns and comments offer direction to the writer.

The best stories are not written — they're rewritten.

During the conferring/rewriting stage children need opportunities to discover whether their writing makes sense, whether it accomplished what they hoped. Using peer and teacher conferences, students can obtain the needed feedback. It is important to focus on content, not mechanics, during the rewriting stage. The real miracle of cooperative learning in the writing process is in the many ways it nurtures the feedback stage of conferring on content. Structures such as Pairs Confer, Teams Confer, Roundtable, Roundrobin, Corners, Inside-Outside Circle, or Numbered Heads Apart lend themselves perfectly to writing conferences.

Again, I emphasize working on the sense of the piece, the content, during the conferring/rewriting stage. Polishing the content for effective and understandable communication is what rewriting is all about. The time for correcting spelling and mechanics does not arrive until the content is ready for publication. Students often think that looking through a piece of writing for misspelled words and needed punctuation is rewriting. It is not. Rewriting is a revision of wording: word choice, transition, sentence structure, and paragraph placement.

It will help students revise if the teacher does not require a story to be recopied during revision. Two ways to achieve this are writing all rough drafts double spaced, or using only one side of the paper so writers can add, or cut and paste.

Teacher-Student Conferencing

Teachers, as well as peers, engage in conferences on content. Nancie Atwell (1987) who writes prolifically on using the writing process in classrooms, looks at content in her classroom by refusing to touch the student's draft, instead looking at faces as students read to her. This holds at bay the English teacher with the slashing red pen who sees only errors. Atwell conducts frequent, brief conferences with students. She initiates the conference with a simple, "How's it coming?" and reserves her suggestions for the areas of concern to the students.

Questions and comments during the conferring/rewriting stage should be planned to elicit thinking in the writer about what he or she needs to do next to make the writing better. Graves (1991) also researched and refined the teacher-student writing conference. He describes it as a brief discussion covering the history of the piece ("Where did this idea come from? Have you tried anything like this before?"), the current status of the piece ("How's it going? Any problems?"), and future plans for the piece ("What will you do next? Who will read this?").

Peer Conferencing

Part of our role as teachers is to help children learn to respond in helpful ways during peer conferences.

- **Corners**
- **Inside-Outside Circle**
- **Numbered Heads**
- **Pairs Confer**
- **Roundrobin**
- **Roundtable**
- **Teams Confer**

Conferencing Structures

> ### Teaching Positive Peer Conferencing
> 1. Use Gambits.
> 2. Use Peer Response Forms.
> 3. Use modeling and reinforcement.

Give students gambits and peer response forms for responding to classmates' writing. See reproducible Peer Conference Gambit Cards, page 14, and Peer Conference Response Form, page 15.

Gambits are sentence openers, which help students learn to speak with each other in a positive way. Sometimes children are well versed in name calling, insults, and put downs, but have no experience delivering positive feedback. You may want to refer to Kagan (1992). He details several structures that help promote positive communication patterns.

Gambits are included on the rough draft reproducible for every lesson in the book as a reminder to both students and teachers that meeting a writer's minimum daily requirement need for positive feedback promotes growth. Teach the use of gambits and response forms as part of the week's work in the area of social skills.

The teacher can model positive conferencing with a student during a whole class discussion. Sitting in front of the class, one author reads his or her story to the teacher as classmates listen. The teacher then uses modeling to demonstrate effective responses to the writing.

The Peer Response Forms, the Gambit Cards, and teacher modeling will quickly bring the students to a level of productive conferencing in small groups. Even first and second graders can be trusted to make productive suggestions during conferences on content with this type of guidance.

Another form of modeling is for the teacher to write WITH the students, and model revisions of his or her own writing. Spill some of your own blood. Your open admission of imperfection, and your willingness to manipulate the words, will help kids see what revision is really about.

Teachers and peers need to be reminded that it is the writer's decision whether to act on suggestions made during conferences on content. William Zinsser (1988) speaks of the transaction between writer and teacher as "sacramental." He reminds us that dealing with students' writing is not just dealing with words, but with the person who wrote the words. For that reason, the author is always the final judge of the writing: what words to choose and what to do with the words.

Editing/Proofreading

Once the author feels that the words tell the reader what the writer wants to say in the clearest way possible, the writer moves into the editing phase of the writing process.

Peers can provide excellent proofreading and editing help for each other. Peer editing should be used before teacher editing. Depending on the student's plans for publication, the teacher may choose not to enter the editing process at all. Proofreading and editing with Pairs Confer, Teams Confer, One Stray, Three Stay, Experts Edit, or Corners provide students opportunities to master the mechanics by using them on real work.

When the teacher edits, he or she might mark only those matters of concern identi-fied by the student. Let the student ask for the type of help wanted. Many early writers may want help with quotation marks or indenting.

"But...what about grammar, mechanics, and spelling?" you ask. Evidence shows that teaching grammar and mechanics in isolation does not produce good writing. Children who produce genuine writing, not worksheet writing, learn grammar and mechanics because they carry important weight. That weight is the burden, and the joy, of communicating well.

Spelling ability grows through the same sort of organic process that produces students fluent in grammar and mechanics. That means that teachers in the early grades can feel comfortable allowing invented spellings. Part of the editing process could be for a student to underline words that he or she thinks are misspelled in every piece of writing. It's powerful when a student recognizes that a word is spelled incorrectly. Help the child learn the word then, when it's needed.

As an adult I have learned the "grammar and mechanics" of several word processing programs. I began with a program for the Commodore, then I learned AppleWorks, and now I am using MacWrite II. When I sat down at the computer to begin learning each of these programs, I had not read the manual from cover to cover and mastered every skill needed to write with the new program. I had the words. I could get the words on the screen, just as a child is able to get words on paper. When I needed the mechanics (How do I change the tabs?

- **Corners**
- **Experts Edit**
- **One Stray**
- **Pairs Confer**
- **Roundtable Edit**
- **Teams Confer**

Editing/Proofreading Structures

Virginia DeBolt: *Write! Cooperative Learning and the Writing Process*

10   Kagan Cooperative Learning • 1 (800) WEE CO-OP

How do I turn off the underlining?) I turned to the manual and learned the one piece of information I needed at the moment. And I remembered it, because I chose to learn it.

If we teach children to use quotation marks when they say to us, "How do I make it show who's talking?" they will remember, too, because they want to know. Rather than learning skills in isolation, students learn mechanics in the context of their struggle to create meaning on the page.

Some teachers choose to have brief lessons on topics related to the writing in progress at the beginning of each class. In that case, the teacher can edit for the one or two skills that he or she is currently teaching. A reproducible chart of editing marks is on page 17.

Writing to Learn   vs.   Reading to Learn

What do you have to say?	**What did they have to say?**
Be active. Do it.	**Sit still. Pay attention.**
Student chooses the words.	**Teacher chooses the words.**
Productive. Output.	**Consumptive. Input.**

Publishing

When the writing is ready to be published it might take many forms: notes pinned to the bulletin board, letters mailed to the President, illustrated stories displayed in the hallways, books bound in protective covers, or reports turned in at the conclusion of a unit in Social Studies. Celebrate the growth and success of students as writers in many ways during the school year. An Author's Party or the ceremonial placing of a student written book in the school library are two of many ways to celebrate publication. Professional publications that accept children's writing are listed in Chapter 25.

Adventure: Writing

Writing is a complex adventure. The writer may be startled to discover that he or she knows and understands things never before articulated. The act of writing clarifies and deepens thinking. Many of us, when faced with an essay question on a test, have felt the awful sensation, "I don't know that." But as we begin to write we realize we do know it — perhaps more than we thought we knew — perhaps with connections we didn't realize we had made. Writing to learn is a trend in education today acknowledging the connections between writing and thinking, writing and learning.

In or Out?

We learn more from output than we learn from input. Teachers, authors of the phrase, "You never really know a subject until you teach it," know this at a subconscious level. If we think about it consciously, as it applies to students and learning, we realize that students learn to write by writing, not by hearing about writing or practicing on the subskills of writing.

"Teachers have discovered," according to Peter Elbow (1990), "that writing is more useful than reading as the entrance into literacy." Writing to learn is powerful for some of the same reasons cooperative learning is powerful. Consider this: Most successful writing programs view writing as a social act. Students talk about story ideas. Students give and receive feedback during all stages of writing. Cooperative Learning provides the atmosphere in which children can safely test their ideas, find their voices as writers, and be heard.

References

Atwell, Nancie. *In the Middle: Writing, Reading, and Learning with Adolescents.* Upper Montclair, New Jersey: Boynton/Cook, 1987.

Elbow, Peter. *What is English?* New York: Modern Language Association of America, 1990.

Graves, Donald H. *Build a Literate Classroom.* Portsmouth, NH: Heinemann, 1991.

Kagan, Spencer. *Cooperative Learning.* San Juan Capistrano, CA: Kagan Cooperative Learning, 1993.

Zinsser, William. *Writing to Learn.* New York: Harper and Row, 1988.

Virginia DeBolt: *Write! Cooperative Learning and the Writing Process*

12   Kagan Cooperative Learning • 1 (800) WEE CO-OP

The Writing Process

Peer Conference Gambit Cards

Directions: Use these sentence beginnings when you respond to the content of a story.

I like the part where...

I like the way you used the word _____.

What did you mean when you said...

What happened after...

I liked your beginning because...

I would like to know more about...

I had a clear picture in my mind of the part where...

What would you lose if...

What are you going to do next?

Peer Conference Response Form

Author's Name _____

Title _____

Helper's Name _____

Date _____

I like

I want to know more about

One thing you might think about doing

Other

10 Rules for Writers

1. Write.

2. Write.

3. Write often.

4. Write about anything.

5. Write about everything.

6. Write about what you see.

7. Write about what you learn.

8. Write about what you think.

9. Write about what you read.

10. WRITE!

Proofreader's Marks

Use these standard marks to show corrections needed in written copy. These symbols are used so that anyone who reads the writing will interpret the corrections in the same way.

¶

(make a new paragraph)

~~order~~ ⌐

(take out)

<u>as she</u>

(capitalize)

some one

(close up space)

∧

(add)

by A

(make lowercase)

thier

(reverse letters or words)

on the

(insert a space)

soup∧nuts

(add punctuation)

because
~~since~~

(change words)

for her

(move as shown)

⊙

(add a period)

Peer Response	Title
	Name

Virginia DeBolt: *Write! Cooperative Learning and the Writing Process*

18   Kagan Cooperative Learning • 1 (800) WEE CO-OP

Peer Response

Title

Name

Virginia DeBolt: *Write! Cooperative Learning and the Writing Process*

Kagan Cooperative Learning • 1 (800) WEE CO-OP   19

Title _____

Name _____

_____

_____

_____

_____

_____

_____

_____

_____

_____

_____

_____

_____

_____

_____

_____

_____

_____

_____

Virginia DeBolt: *Write! Cooperative Learning and the Writing Process*

20   Kagan Cooperative Learning • 1 (800) WEE CO-OP

Title

Name

Virginia DeBolt: *Write! Cooperative Learning and the Writing Process*
Kagan Cooperative Learning • 1 (800) WEE CO-OP

21

Evaluating Students' Writing

The Medium is the Message

Metacommunications

The evaluation method a teacher chooses communicates his or her attitude regarding writing to the students. Analytic scoring communicates that students write in order to receive a grade. Holistic scoring bears some kinship to grading, but can be adapted to communicate concern for and appreciation of what is done well, and to include student input. Primary trait scoring, when tied to a specific lesson, can be viewed as a learning device. Portfolio evaluation communicates to the student that he or she is a writer in the process of creating a large body of work which will demonstrate efforts, progress, and achievement over the school year. Students who evaluate themselves in the Learner's Journal receive the message that writing is a way to understand themselves and their learning. Peer evaluation in revising and editing conferences communicates the idea that writing is a process enhanced by feedback.

Access

Learners who write in a cooperative learning environment have frequent opportunities for self evaluation and peer evaluation. They are learners with access — access to effective experience with the writing process, and access to growth in writing and thinking through their active participation as writers and critiquers of writing.

Evaluation Media
Portfolio Evaluation

Let's take a closer look at each of the evaluation media, beginning with portfolio evaluation. A classroom using portfolios has several characteristics. There are frequent opportunities to write in many ways and about many topics. The student is regarded as someone who has something to say about his or her learning and growth as a writer.

Portfolio Evaluation
Student is a writer in process of creating a large body of work which will demonstrate efforts, progress, and achievement.

Holistic
Can be adapted to reflect what is done well and to include student input.

Primary Trait Scoring
Students receive a grade based on one characteristic of their writing. Can be viewed as a learning device when tied to a specific lesson.

Analytic
Students write to receive a grade.

Self (Learner's Journal)
Writing is a way to understand yourself and your learning.

Peer Evaluation
A writers' workshop atmosphere is created.

Evaluation Mediums

Two portfolios are maintained, distinguished here as the "Working Folder" and the "Assessment Portfolio." Stapled to the four surfaces of the Working Folder are four sheets where the student records ideas and accomplishments. See reproducibles on pages 28-31.

Things I Know. One sheet lists topics about which the student knows a great deal. These lists are as individual as the students themselves and can range from archery to zookeeping. The purpose of this list is to help the student see himself or herself as a source of knowledge and ideas, and to realize that such knowledge can become a writing topic.

Ideas to Write About. The second sheet stapled to the writing folder is used to list new ideas to write about. It might include events in the student's life, books or movies worthy of comment, poem possibilities, characters or settings for future stories. This list prevents future writing ideas from being lost or forgotten. As the student finishes one project, the list can be examined for a new idea.

Titles of Finished Writing. Third, a sheet bearing a list of finished pieces is attached to the working folder.

Skills I Have Mastered.
The fourth sheet enumerates the student's growth in editing, proofreading, grammar, sentence structure, paragraphing and other mechanics. Once a skill is mastered to the degree that it is included on the list of accomplishments, a student is expected to continue using it correctly. The

student and teacher together decide what is included on the skills mastered sheet.

The folders should be kept in boxes or files in a classroom location accessible to both students and teacher. Keeping the working folders in a box will preserve them in better condition than allowing students to keep them in their desks. All papers connected with the work in progress are kept in the working folder. Even little scraps of paper with choice words, great thoughts, jokes, rhymes, and questions can be saved as working draft material. When a piece is finished it is dated, and all the original drafts and the final copy are saved in the folder.

Near the end of each grading period, the student chooses two pieces for the Assessment Portfolio. There must be sufficient quantity in the folder from which to choose. Requiring at least one finished draft each week would result in six selections from which to choose during a six-week grading period. The two selected pieces represent what the student considers to be his/her best work for the six weeks. The writing grade will be based on evidence of the student's growth and progress as shown in the two best works. At year's end, the student's portfolio will contain his or her 12 best, dated throughout the year.

The student's written explanation telling why he or she selected the two particular pieces for evaluation can be included in either the Learner's Journal or the Assessment Portfolio. Requiring such an assessment from the student provides him or her with the opportunity to cite reasons why a

> **Writing Skills I Can Use Correctly**
> 1. *Period at the end of a sentence*
> 2. *Capitalize names*
> 3. *Commas in a series*
> 4.
> 5.
> 6.
> 7.
> 8.

I picked the poem about my baby brother as one of my two best pieces because I've always had trouble with poems. It was pretty hard to make it rhyme. That's why I think it shows my progress.

particular piece is significant in demonstrating growth or progress.

After each six weeks the working folders can be emptied of work. (The student who is in mid-project should, of course, keep needed work in the folder.) Save this "old" work in a drawer or box, in case a student needs to refer to some previous work. You never know when January's flash of genius will solve a writing problem left behind in October.

Holistic Scoring

Holistic scoring is used frequently in scoring commercially produced writing assessment tests. It responds to the writing as a whole. Reliable results are obtained in holistic scoring by using a series of readers. Scales ranging from 1-4 or 1-6 points are popular. Holistic scoring can reward the student for what is done well.

The scoring guide needs to be specific to both the work assigned and the level of ability of the writers. If students are permitted to participate in creating the scoring guide, holistic scoring can be empowering to the student. The act of defining the requirements for excellence in, for example, research reports or personal narratives, gives students perspective into what is expected and possible. It enables students to utilize a minute-by-minute evaluation of their work and their peers' work throughout the writing process.

The movement in the field of English toward process and away from teaching isolated skills supports the need to measure writing as a whole unit of expression. Holistic evaluation weighs the merits of individual thought more than mere correctness.

A general purpose Holistic Scoring Guide can be found on page 32.

Primary Trait Scoring

Primary trait scoring, or single focus scoring, is useful following instruction in a particular skill. Suppose, for example, that the students were learning to use dialog in stories, and the teacher had presented a lesson on quotation marks. A holistic score of 1-4 would be assigned to a student's writing based on the single trait of quotation marks. The teacher responds to the work as a whole and does not search meticulously for places to pen in red quotation marks on the student's paper. Students earning 1's or 2's might be grouped for additional help. Students earning 4's can add quotation marks to their list of skills mastered. The children earning the 4's might become the expert editors for the writing projects requiring dialogue and quotation marks.

Analytic Scoring

Analytic scoring is used in an effort to assign grades to writing based on subskills. It uses a weighted scale which can be altered to fit the writing style. For example, a research report might be scored for its bibliography, a poem for meter and rhyme. The Analytic Scoring reproducible on page 34 can serve for many types of writing.

Drawbacks of Analytic Scoring!

There is little agreement on the definition or importance of the various subskills. Nor is there evidence showing that the accumulation of a set of subskills will lead to quality writing. Another major drawback with analytic scoring is its unreliability. Scores assigned by one teacher may be different or even contradict those assigned by another teacher.

Teachers who want to use analytic scoring, despite its drawbacks, can adapt the general guide to give weight to specific items required in particular assignments or writing styles. In writing stories, for example, points might be earned for effective use of setting, character, conflict, and plot resolution. Make it work for you. If you are undeterred by the drawbacks and really want to use analytic scoring, then let the students design it. Otherwise, analytic scoring is of little value.

Self Evaluation

The Learner's Journal is an appropriate place for students to reflect on their own writing and on their progress as writers. Self evaluation is inherent in Portfolio Assessment, described above. If writing is considered a process of refinement and improvement, students will evaluate their every idea, word, and sentence from the first blush of thought to the last period on a final draft. Self evaluation gives students a stake in their own growth as thinkers and learners.

Peer Evaluation

During rewriting, conferring, proofreading, and editing activities students help one another while discussing questions such as, "Is the meaning clear?" and, "What could I do to make my writing better?" Peer evaluation allows students to generate and critique options, and thus becomes an experience in learning and applying effective thinking and writing skills. A writers' workshop atmosphere is created with the use of peer evaluation.

The Teacher's Daily Response to Writing

Use these lessons not once, but many times. Don't write just one poem, one story, one editorial. Provide students with many opportunities to write. Teach them responses and gambits for positive peer conferences. Amass evidence of student's growth as writers in folders and portfolios. Plan minilessons on the mechanics and conventions of written language. Then, interact daily with students about their progress.

That daily interaction occurs in three basic ways: in brief student-teacher writing conferences with a few students each day, as an ongoing dialog in the students' Learner's Journals, and in the nightly reading and evaluation of four or five students' folders. It isn't necessary to read every child's writing folder each day. Keep track of

Virginia DeBolt: *Write! Cooperative Learning and the Writing Process*

26   Kagan Cooperative Learning • 1 (800) WEE CO-OP

progress, lessons needed, and potential areas of growth for each student. Communicate your involvement and appreciation for their unique experiences and unique mode of expression.

References

Graves, Donald H. *Writing: Teachers and Children at Work.* Portsmouth, New Hampshire, Heinemann Educational Books, 1983.

Haley-James, Shirley, et al. *Houghton Mifflin English.* Boston, Houghton Mifflin Company, 1988.

Rief, Linda. "Finding the Value in Evaluation: Self-Assessment in the Middle School Classroom." *Educational Leadership,* Vol. 47, March 1990.

White, Edward M. *Teaching and Assessing Writing.* San Francisco, Jossey-Bass Publishers, 1985.

Things I Know About

1. _____
2. _____
3. _____
4. _____
5. _____
6. _____
7. _____
8. _____
9. _____
10. _____
11. _____
12. _____
13. _____
14. _____
15. _____
16. _____
17. _____
18. _____
19. _____
20. _____

Need more space? Add a new sheet!

Ideas to Write About

1. _____

2. _____

3. _____

4. _____

5. _____

6. _____

7. _____

8. _____

9. _____

10. _____

11. _____

12. _____

13. _____

14. _____

15. _____

16. _____

17. _____

18. _____

19. _____

20. _____

Need more space? Add a new sheet!

Virginia DeBolt: *Write! Cooperative Learning and the Writing Process*
Kagan Cooperative Learning • 1 (800) WEE CO-OP

29

Titles of my Finished Writing

1. _____
2. _____
3. _____
4. _____
5. _____
6. _____
7. _____
8. _____
9. _____
10. _____
11. _____
12. _____
13. _____
14. _____
15. _____
16. _____
17. _____
18. _____
19. _____
20. _____

Need more space? Add a new sheet!

Writing Skills I Can Use Correctly

1. _____

2. _____

3. _____

4. _____

5. _____

6. _____

7. _____

8. _____

9. _____

10. _____

11. _____

12. _____

13. _____

14. _____

15. _____

16. _____

17. _____

18. _____

19. _____

20. _____

Holistic Scoring Guide

 The writing demonstrates a clearly developed plan. It includes details that describe and explain. The message is clear with well developed ideas. There are few or no spelling or mechanical errors.

 The writing fulfills the assignment. It is competently organized and developed. Sequence is less controlled and there is less elaboration than in the 4 quality writing. There are a few spelling or mechanical errors.

 The writing has organizational gaps. The vocabulary is general and lacking in detail. The message is not conveyed clearly, although the reader has a general idea what the writer is trying to say. Frequent lapses in logic and spelling or mechanical errors may interfere with meaning.

 There is little or no sequence and attention to detail. The writer addresses the assignment only indirectly. Gross errors in sentence construction, spelling or mechanics make the meaning unclear or incoherent.

Virginia DeBolt: *Write! Cooperative Learning and the Writing Process*
Kagan Cooperative Learning • 1 (800) WEE CO-OP

32

Sample

Analytic Scoring

	Poor	Weak	Fair	Good	Excellent
Content	4	8	12	16	20
Organization		8			
Elaboration				16	
Language			12		
Mechanics	2	4	6	8	10
Capitals				8	
Spelling					10
Punctuation					10
Final Draft	2	4	6	8	10
Legibility & format				8	

Total Score ___72___

Letter Grade ___C___

Analytic Scoring

	Poor	Weak	Fair	Good	Excellent
Content Organization Elaboration Language	4	8	12	16	20
Mechanics Capitals Spelling Punctuation	2	4	6	8	10
Final Draft Legibility & format	2	4	6	8	10

Total Score _____

Letter Grade _____

Virginia DeBolt: *Write! Cooperative Learning and the Writing Process*
Kagan Cooperative Learning • 1 (800) WEE CO-OP

34

The Structures

Cooperative Learning lessons are composed of structures. Structures have no content in and of themselves. Teachers add whatever content they consider appropriate to the structures. In other words, structures are used over and over again. Students could brainstorm with Roundtable one day and use Roundtable to proofread the following day. A structure plus content equals a learning activity. The lessons in this book are multi-structural, that is, they consist of a series of learning activities leading to the accomplishment of a goal.

Most of the structures used in this volume are cloned from Kagan's Structural Approach. A few I invented to deal with the needs of process writing activities. Some of these "inventions" are not truly structures—for example, the Read In—but are labeled as structures because of the organization of the book.

I see Spencer Kagan as the Synthesizer of Cooperative Learning. He studies the work of researchers, psychologists and educators. He weaves it together in his Structural Approach and creates a refined system both valuable and workable in the classroom. He's a Master: his work is philosophically thoughtful and eminently practical.

Descriptions of the structures found in this chapter are general in nature. Uses are suggested, but don't feel limited by the suggestions. If you want to review a structure, to check on whether a particular structure would work with content you have in mind, or read a quick description of an unfamiliar structure, this chapter is designed to help you.

Notice that the structures are listed alphabetically so that you can locate each one quickly. Also notice that in describing the structures and their uses, I have assumed that you are working with "ideal" teams of four. I know that out in the trenches you have teams of three, or five, or six. We're flexible — put three in a "pair" or five in a "square."

The charts on pages II-VI will help you locate specific structures in the lesson designs, and specific uses for structures within the writing process.

Author's Party
Publishing

An Authors' Party is a celebration and sharing of students' writings. Guests are invited and welcomed. Use the Author's Award reproducible to recognize students for creativity, improvement, best writing, best poem, humorous writing, good researching, best mystery, and other such achievements. Have students give readings of all or parts of their work. Reproduce individual or class books and have a book signing so that guests may leave with an autographed copy of the work being celebrated. Serve refreshments. Good food and good writing: now that's a party!

Book It
Publishing

Book It is a celebration of students' work published in book form. Take the students' best work--any size, shape, genre, or length of writing--and bind it in durable covers as a book. The work of individual writers can be bound as separate books. Class members can contribute to bound anthologies. The books can be shared in a Read In, placed in the school or classroom library, given as gifts, sent by traveling "bookmobile" to other classes for reading, or kept by the writers. You will find suggestions for book binding in Chapter 25.

Carbon Sharing
Proofreading/Editing

Carbon Sharing is a method of creating multiple copies of students' work. Several peer helpers examine the piece simultaneously and confer on comments for the author.

Using carbon paper or the photocopier, students make several copies of their revised first draft. The work can then be simultaneously proofread and edited by the writer's teammates or classmates. The writer receives several students' editing ideas in a brief time. After looking over the edited copies, the writer will understand where corrections need to be made. If there is disagreement among the student proofreaders and editors, the writer can request a conference with the teacher. This is when the teacher points out the English Handbook, smiles and walks away. Let the students have a chance to put their heads together and find the solution before you step into the process.

Chalkboard Share
Prewriting

Chalkboard Share is a variety of Simultaneous Sharing wherein each team sends a representative to the board to share or display something the team has accomplished. Each team has a designated space on the chalkboard marked and labeled with the team name. In this volume, Chalkboard Share is used to display proper letter format. See page 102.

Chalkboard Share is also an effective way to follow up a Numbered Heads Together activity on mechanics of English such as correct spellings of verbs or homonyms, capitalization of titles, or capitalization of proper nouns.

Class Brainstorming
Prewriting

Class Brainstorming invites every member of a class to share in a brainstorming activity. A recorder, possibly the teacher, writes ideas on the chalkboard as students call them out. As with small group brainstorming, fluency is encouraged by asking students to get silly, to think quickly, to build on the ideas of others, and to suspend judgment. You might choose to set a time limit: "Let's brainstorm for five minutes and see how many fairy tales we can name that use three's in the plot or in numbers of characters."

Class Discussion

Prewriting, Conferring/ Rewriting, Publishing

A whole Class Discussion is an effective technique for developing an anticipatory set prior to beginning a writing project or assignment. During the revising stage of the writing process, a Class Discussion is useful in helping students refine their thinking or writing. It can have a synergistic effect on thinking; that is, students who have done preliminary writing on a subject might find a new connection or a direction for new writing from ideas that come from classmates. If you have a team product-- only one piece of writing per team--the Class Discussion is useful for sharing the work. Couple the sharing of a team product with evaluation using a class generated holistic evaluation scale and you have a powerful learning experience to use before students write independently.

Class Value Line

A Class Value Line is a method of demonstrating a value judgment by standing in a position on an imaginary line. The imaginary line represents the students' attitudes of agreement, disagreement, neutralilty, or indecisiveness about a statement. The statement is one open to value judgment. For example: "Schools should do away with all standardized testing," or, "We should help

the hungry in our own country before we send aid anywhere else."

Co-op Co-op

Co-op Co-op is a structure for division of labor. Multi-task assignments and responsibilities related to an overall theme or project allow for a diversity of interests. Higher order thinking skills are used to synthesize and present learning.

The Co-op Co-op lesson design touches every aspect of the writing process. In Co-op Co-op, students engage in creative investigation, determining for themselves the content of their studies, the way in which to study, the way in which to record, organize and present their own learning, and the way in which to best synthesize, organize, and present the learning of the team. In this volume, Co-op Co-op is used for Research Reports and A School Newspaper. It could also be used for investigating and writing about topics in science, social studies, music, and across-curriculum theme based units. Opportunity for diversity and creativity in the written product of a Co-op Co-op project is unlimited. Wildlife field guides, illuminated manuscripts, and plays are a few of many possibilities.

As defined by Kagan (1992), there are ten steps of Co-op Co-op.
1. Student-centered class discussion designed to stimulate student curiosity.
2. Selection of student teams for maximum heterogeneity according to gender, ethnicity and ability.
3. Team building and skill development to develop bonding, or the will to cooperate, and to develop the skills needed to cooperate on the tasks or goals.

4. Team topic selection allows the teams to focus on one aspect of the learning unit as a whole.
5. Mini-topic selection by individual teammembers allows students to focus on one aspect of the team topic. Topic selections are subject to the teacher's approval.
6. Mini-topic preparation by individual students can include interviews, surveys, observations, and experiments.
7. Mini-topic presentations are made by individual students to their teams. There is usually a time for feedback and further preparation by individuals, if it is needed.
8. Preparation of team presentations entail the synthesis of the mini-topic material into a team demonstration that should aim to be more than just the sum of its parts.
9. Team presentations are made to the whole class. Non-lecture formats are preferred.
10. Reflection and evaluation is sought from individuals, teams, the class, and the teacher. Individual mini-topic presentations are evaluated by teammates, team presentations are evaluated by classmates, and each individual is also evaluated by the teacher. Students should develop evaluation and reflection forms as part of the project.

Corners

Conferring/Rewriting,
Proofreading/Editing
Corners are used to create temporary teams or groupings of students based on interest or need.

In Corners, each corner of the room represents a particular topic or skill. For ex-

ample, students move to one corner of the room for help on punctuation, another for spelling, another for capitalization and yet another for paragraphing. Or the corners might represent genres — science fiction writers meet in one corner, poets in another, playwrights in another, and mystery writers in the fourth. Corners can hold writing conferences on aspects of the school newspaper — articles, editorials, ads, features. Students choose their corner based on need or interest. While working in the corner, a student may interact with one or several other students. A conference on content might be held with students in each corner in a circle: all the students in a particular corner cooperate as a critique group. A Corners editing conference, on the other hand, might be more effective with students in each corner working in pair groups.

Cube-It Brainstorming

Prewriting
Students make a small paper cube, the sides of which are inscribed with prompts or words intended to promote elaboration and fluency during prewriting.

Cubing is a way of examining a problem or situation from six sides. Students cut out a paper cube and paste it together to hold as they brainstorm. In the Poetry lesson design, (see page 83) the cube elicits sensory and emotional output. On the other hand, the Editorial Writing lesson design (see page 175) uses Cubing to examine an issue and take a position for or against it. The teacher can choose words for the cube that are reflective of the type of writing undertaken. A blank cube pattern reproducible is included for you to reproduce. See page 84.

Descriptive Spiders

Prewriting

The "spider" is a visual matrix for the elaboration of ideas. By adding details on "legs" around an oval "body" of ideas, the student creates a spider-like web of ideas.

To help a reader translate writing into a vivid visual experience, the writer adds details that appeal to the senses. The Descriptive Spiders activity helps each student develop ideas and vocabulary to better communicate the sensory in their writing.

Descriptive spiders work as individual brainstorming aids, or as team Roundtable activities. There is a master in Chapter 6 for a handout for this activity that teachers may adapt to meet the needs of fiction writers. The teacher may ask the writers to fill in the circles with character names and add traits of those characters to the spider's legs. Or, the teacher may tell the students to brainstorm synonyms, action verbs, or adjectives using the spiders in a roundtable. In Chapter 13, a descriptive spider handout elicits sensory detail.

The descriptive spider is versatile. Students can:

- Put names of characters in the circles and fill in traits and attributes about characterization around the "spider's legs."
- Put items for comparison in the circles and write similarities and differences around the outside.
- Put frequently used words in the circles and add synonyms to the legs.

Draw-What-I-Write

Prewriting

This structure is useful in focusing attention on the importance of precision in wording or language.

Each student draws a simple picture, working alone away from teammates, and then writes a paragraph describing the drawing. Students return to teams and work in pairs, exchanging written descriptions. Teammates attempt to reproduce the drawing using only the paragraph.

Experts Edit

Proofreading/Editing

Student experts work with teammates and classmates in Experts Edit. Peer cooperation as proofreaders and editors benefits both writers and helpers. Arrange work spaces in the corners of the room for the student editors. As the writers complete revisions and are ready for proofreading or editing help, they move to the appropriate editor. The student editor might be a handy-dandy-all-purpose-helper, or might be a specialist in one skill such as capitalization. Cross age tutoring fits this structure. Why not, for example, invite fourth graders into the first grade to set up shop in the corners of the room to help as expert editors?

Find-Someone-Who...

Prewriting

In Find-Someone-Who, students move around the room at random searching for someone who has whatever information or material is sought. In Chapter 18, Find-Someone-Who is used to help students form teams of the 5 W's of the lead paragraph: Who, What, Where, When, Why (sometimes How).

As a Classbuilding activity, Find-Some-one-Who helps students get acquainted. It is an active and entertaining way to find interview partners, conduct surveys, or create temporary random teams.

Formations
Prewriting

Formations move in the realm of kines-thetic or whole body involvement. Words, sentences, letters, numbers, and more are "formed" by the students. A "no talking rule" is in-teresting to use in For-mations. For example, a team might be asked to create a Formation of an active verb without talking to each other about it.

Using their bodies as building mate-rial, students create Formations. Formations are used in the letter writing lesson design, page 104. "If the gym floor were a big letter, and you were the comma after the closing, where would you stand?" When everyone is in place, the letter "reads" itself out loud.

Formations can be used in English skills development in other ways. Make one child a noun, one a verb, one a direct ob-ject, another an article, and so on. Instruct them to form themselves into a sentence. Or have students form the commas be-tween articles in a series.

Free Write
Prewriting

Each individual works alone during Free Write. There are no rules to follow. There is no requirement as to correct spelling, capitalization, or punctuation. It is a form of free association or solo brainstorming wherein the writer attempts to record the contents of his or her thinking as quickly as possible. Free Write loosens or frees the writer's thoughts and imagination. Later, after unleashing his or her words in Free Write, the writer returns to the page to organize, evaluate, and assemble the ideas into a coherent first draft. A great practice during Free Write is to set a time limit, say 10 minutes, and insist that the student write without stopping for the entire time. Students write until they think they've said it all, but if they must continue writing anyway, they often break loose all sorts of wonderful insights and surprises.

Guess-the-Fib
Prewriting

This structure provides opportu-nities for team building, consen-sus building and improvement in interviewing. Students take turns at stumping teammates with a fib.

Students state two facts and one fib about themselves. Teammates come to con-sensus as to which state-ment they think is the fib. If the guess is incorrect, an-other chance is given. Students can use Guess-the-Fib in giving book reports, in planning interview stories, in reviewing literature familiar, and in learning new things about teammates during team building activities.

Independent Writing
Writing

Independent Writing is at the heart of every writing assignment. Each writer must finally sit alone with pencil and paper to choose and arrange the words. The writer is responsible for deciding what to say and how to say it during this time. Tools for writers — the thesaurus, the dictionary, the English handbook — should be readily available.

Individual Interviews
Prewriting

For a one-on-one interview, students learn to preplan questions and take notes. Interview information is used in many writing assignments including news reports, biographies, profiles, and introductions.

Inside-Outside Circle
Prewriting, Conferring/ Rewriting
Inside-Outside Circle pairs up students briefly. Then circles rotate and new pairs

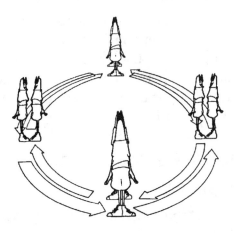

are formed. Teams of two or four can rotate within the circles to interact briefly with other teams.

Students leave their desks and face each other in two concentric circles, one inside the other, for Inside-Outside Circle. While arranged in this way, students talk in pairs or groups of four. Then the circles rotate, providing each child with a new partner with whom to talk. Used early in the writing process, the talk can generate ideas during prewriting. If students have written a first draft, they carry it with them to the Inside-Outside Circle. Pairing up, the writers read their first drafts and ask for comments and suggestions. Then the circles rotate and first drafts are read again for another reaction. After a few rotations, the young writer will learn where his or her first draft is well written, where it is unclear, where it is incomplete, and what needs to be done during rewriting. Team Inside-Outside Circle can be also used to rehearse skits or share team projects.

Jigsaw
Prewriting/Writing/Publishing
Jigsaw is a design for division of labor. It is used in two lessons in this book: Skits and Plays and School Newspapers. There are numerous variations of Jigsaw. (see the 1992 edition of Kagan's *Cooperative Learning* for 15 pages devoted to Jigsaw variations. In the basic Jigsaw design, each student on the team specializes in one aspect of a project and becomes the team expert on one part of the learning. The teammates share their expertise, putting their efforts

together in a combined product. A team of four or more could write and perform a play using Jigsaw. In producing a school newspaper, the whole class could divide to form various expert groups in a Jigsaw design.

Magic Cards

Prewriting

This "magic" selection process helps the undecided pick a topic.

If a student is undecided about a topic, or word choice, or title, Magic Cards can be one way of choosing. In pairs, students select five possibilities. Story ideas can be taken from a student's list of ideas to write about. A pair of writers could brainstorm five possible titles. The possibilities are written on cards. The undecided student turns away, while his or her partner places the alternatives face down on the desk and mixes them. Turning back, the first student holds his hand above the cards, waving them in the air until the magic emanations from the cards pull his hand down the one particular card. The student picks up that card and thus the choice is made as to the day's topic or the story's title.

Mix-Freeze-Group

Prewriting/Conferring/Rewriting/ Publishing

Mix-Freeze-Group is a method of forming random teams of various sizes in a few seconds.

Children walk around the room, mixing themselves together in random ways until the teacher says, "Freeze." The teacher sets group size after each freeze. If the teacher says, "Form groups with as many members as there are in a set of twins," students form pairs with whomever is nearby. To create

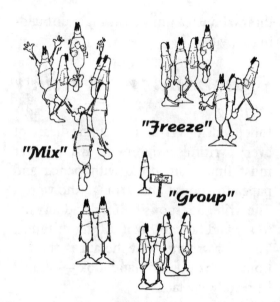

groups of four, the teacher would say something like, "Form groups with as many members as there are legs on a dog."

Mix-Freeze-Group is useful in forming random groups for a specific task. It can also be used in a repeating series of mixing-freezing-and-grouping, pairing up students with someone new at every turn. It's fast, it's fun, and it's active for reviewing, interviewing, sharing, and classbuilding.

Mix-Freeze-Pair

Prewriting

In Mix-Freeze-Pair, students know in advance that they will form pairs when they hear, "Freeze." Use it to form random pairs for book reports, for listening and sharing stories or poems, for surveys, or to review irregular verbs.

Numbered Heads Apart

Conferring/Rewriting/Proofreading/ Editing

Numbered Heads Apart separates a team. The value to writers is that the student's work is read by someone new to the piece,

Virginia DeBolt: *Write! Cooperative Learning and the Writing Process*

42   Kagan Cooperative Learning • 1 (800) WEE CO-OP

someone who doesn't already understand from prewriting activities what the writer is trying to say. The teacher might separate the team by saying, "All the One's meet in this corner, the Two's in that corner," and so on. Or, the teacher might say, "One's, pair up with another One from the nearest team. Two's pair up with the nearest Two," and so on. Another Numbered Heads Apart strategy involves Mix-Freeze-Group. The teacher says, "All the One's mix." The teacher announces, "Freeze. Now form groups with as many members as there are blind mice." These new groups find a place to work as the teacher separates the Two's, Three's, and Four's in similar fashion.

One Stray

Proofreading/Editing
One teammember moves temporarily to a new team, while three teammembers stay behind and work with an incoming "stray" from another team. Taking turns straying and staying behind allows each student an opportunity to temporarily interact with three new teammates.

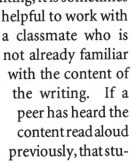

During proofreading and editing, it is sometimes helpful to work with a classmate who is not already familiar with the content of the writing. If a peer has heard the content read aloud previously, that student as editor may not be as attuned to the visual cues in the written language as an unfamiliar reader might be. One Stray, Three Stay allows each team member, in turn, to stray to a new team with a revised first draft ready for proofreading and editing. With Roundtable editing or, if car-

bons or photocopies are used, with simultaneous editing, the new team helps the writer achieve an improved version of the writing. Everyone returns to the home team, and another set of students stray, until all four team members have strayed and returned.

Pairs Compare

Prewriting
After completing a pair assignment, two sets of pairs unite to compare results. Pairs work together to compare and evaluate

ideas generated during prewriting activities. Pairs Compare is useful in analyzing positions taken on an issue by comparing ideas from two points of view.

Pairs Confer

Conferring/Rewriting,
Proofreading/Editing
Conferring in pairs to rewrite, proofread, and edit the students' work is the simplest method of accomplishing the job. Working in pairs eliminates the need for every child to complete a draft or a revision at a particular time because students can pair up and share their work as they are ready to move to the next step. Pairs Confer can be among teammates, or among classmates. Students can be paired according to criteria the teacher deems necessary at any given moment. Two people and a piece of writ-

ing are the only ingredients necessary for a writing or editing conference. Pairs Confer is a basic structure in the cooperative approach to the writing process.

Pairs Consult

Conferring/Rewriting

In Pairs Consult, students consult each other about their independent work on a pairs assignment. (This is similar to Kagan's Pairs Check.) Each student does the assignment, or part of the assignment, independently. Then the two consult and correct, if need be.

Pairs Consult is suggested for use in the Learner's Journal lesson design. Two students are asked to carry out a task. Each of them has written an approach to the task independently. The two consult with each other to be sure they understand the other's approach and method before undertaking the task. Pairs Consult could be used with student helpers who are outstanding at a particular skill, for example, illustrating or spelling. The helpers could serve as "consultants" for their classmates.

Pairs Debate

Conferring/Rewriting

In a debate, each student takes a position and lists arguments in support of that position. Each debater hopes to persuade listeners or readers to accept his or her point of view. Pairs Debate is used to help students evaluate positions and clarify points in support of a position when conferring on the content of a piece of persuasive writing. Strengths and weaknesses identified in the debate process offer the writer guidance in rewriting for greater persuasive power.

Pair Discussion

Prewriting

The most basic cooperative activity in writing is two students discussing ideas, content, organization, word choice, punctuation, and other aspects of their work.

Pairs Edit

Proofreading/Editing

In pair groups, students work together on editing and proofreading previously revised pieces of writing. While student A edits the work of student B, student B is simultaneously editing the work of student A.

Pairs Experiment

Conferring/Rewriting

Pairs Experiment is a way to test whether or not a piece of writing achieves a particular aim. Have the students written a plan for measuring the height of the flagpole? They experiment in pairs to do what the writing suggests. Have the students written directions for making S'mores? They experiment in pairs to follow the directions. Have the students written directions telling how to find a bag of gum somewhere in the school? They experiment in pairs to follow the directions and find the gum. The activity of carrying out the written plan will help students learn how effective their writing is, and guide them in the rewriting process.

Virginia DeBolt: *Write! Cooperative Learning and the Writing Process*

Kagan Cooperative Learning • 1 (800) WEE CO-OP

44

Pairs Rehearse

Conferring

This structure is useful in preparing a solo performance such as delivering a speech or reading a story aloud to students in lower grades. As one student rehearses, a partner offers help on posture, speaking voice, volume and so on.

Partners

Prewriting/Writing

Half the teammates learn half of what the teams needs to know, while the remaining teammates learn the other half. The teammates then work together as Partners to master the entirety of the information. Partners is a collaborative process with built-in positive interdependence.

In Partners, teams are split into sets of partners. The partners are then separated into two groups. The classroom reforms into two large groups. One partner group receives certain information while the other partner group receives different information. Partners remain separated and work with others who share their information to master the material and prepare to teach the material to the other partner upon returning to their team. When the teams reunite, partners present and tutor. The team then synthesizes information and prepares to use it in a collaborative writing project.

The Partners design, developed by Kagan, (1992, p. 18:2) is extremely powerful for two reasons. It motivates learning more effectively than any teaching method I have experienced. It creates a sense of positive interdependence among teammates because each student has a unique contribution to make to the learning goal.

The steps of Partners, as described by Kagan are:

1. Partners are formed within teams. Often the high and low achiever are partners, as are the two middle achievers.
2. Class divides: partners sit together. Topic 1 partners are all on one side of the class; Topic 2's on the other.
3. Materials are distributed. Materials often consist of some reading and a worksheet. Worksheets are designed to stimulate higher-level thinking.
4. Students master materials.
5. Partners consult with same topic partners. Partners consult with other partners sitting next to them; they check for correctness, completeness, and different points of view.
6. Partners prepare to present and tutor. Partners analyze critical features and decide on a teaching strategy; students are encouraged to make visuals and other teaching aids; they must evaluate what is important to teach, and how to determine if learning has occurred in their teammates.
7. Teams reunite; partners present and tutor. Partners work as a team, dividing the labor as they teach the other partner in their team. After presenting material, partners check for understanding and tutor their teammates. Practice is distributed: Topic 1 partners share, Topic 2 partners share; Topic 1 partners tutor, then, finally, Topic 2 partners tutor.
8. Individual assessment. An individual quiz or essay, or Numbered Heads Together is used to assess individual mastery.

9. Team processing. Teammates reflect back over the process: How did we do as teachers? as learners? How could we do better next time? What social skills did we use? Which should we use next time?

10. Scoring and Recognition. An optional step, often not included, is to have some form or scoring and/or recognition system. The scoring system can be based on student improvement. The recognition system can recognize individual, team, or class accomplishments.

Poetry Reading

Publishing

A Poetry Reading is an act of recognition and celebration. Students read selections of their own poetry aloud to classmates, parents, or invited guests. Videotape the students as they read. Have a reception with punch and cookies afterwards. Poetry with punch!

Rallytable

Writing

Rallytable is similar to Roundtable, but it involves pairs. One paper is passed back and forth between the pair for written work. Young writers can exchange letters, journals, critiques, and more this way.

Read In

Publishing

The main business of a Read In is silent reading. Students' written books and stories are passed around to be read by others. Read Ins can last an hour, half a day, or an entire day. A Read In is suggested for the Biography writing lesson herein, with the subjects of the biographies to be included as guests.

Ceremonies of various sorts can follow a Read In. If the subjects of biographies are there as guests, honor them in some way. An author's awards ceremony could be conducted after the class has read all the books or stories: perhaps a Best Mystery Award, a Best Dialog Award, or a Best Editorial Award might be presented. Students might write book reports about other student's books. Students might write in their Learner's Journal about something learned from reading the work of other students.

Roam the Room

Publishing

Roam the Room is a structure for the simultaneous sharing of written work. The entire class slowly circulates around the room. While roaming, students read the work of other individuals or teams. When individuals are once again seated with teammates, do a Roundrobin to share what was learned.

When writing is completed and ready to be published, each student leaves the final copy on his or her desktop. The members of the class leave their desks and roam the room, silently reading classmates' stories. A blank sheet of paper beside each piece of writing provides a place for recording praise and congratulations from the readers.

Rotating Feedback

Conferring/Rewriting, Publishing

Very like Roam the Room, Rotating Feedback is a structure for the simultaneous sharing of team work. Students travel from display to display as a team, remaining in each area for a prescribed length of time.

Tack or tape the students' work on the walls of the classroom. Under each piece of writing add a blank sheet of paper. During the Rotating Feedback, students leave their desks and stroll around the room, reading the material attached to the walls. Feedback is written by the touring readers on the blank sheets. If the Rotating Feedback is being used in the Conferring/Rewriting stage of the writing process, the feedback should provide praise, suggestions, questions, and hints for the author's consideration in rewriting.

If Rotating Feedback is being used during the publication phase of the writing process, the feedback sheet should be used for congratulations, praise, and celebration. If each team carries a different colored marker as they rotate, the comments on the feedback sheet will be color coded by team.

Roundrobin

Conferring/Rewriting

In a Roundrobin, each child on a team speaks in turn. It effectively insures equal participation and structures in the belief that each team member is equally important. During the writing conference, each student reads his or her first draft aloud to team-mates, who then offer feedback in a Roundrobin. Gambits encouraging positive criticism are useful, especially if students are just beginning to learn to confer on content during the writing process. You will find some suggested gambits on page 14.

Roundtable

Prewriting

Roundtable is a written version of Roundrobin. One sheet of paper is passed from desk to desk so that students make contributions in turn. Roundtable can be used for the generation of ideas, and for the reading or proofing of written work.

In prewriting with Roundtable, teams are given a question or topic about which to think as they pass a large paper from desk to desk. Suppose the teacher wanted students to write a poem about a marshmallow. She could hand each student a marshmallow to study during Roundtable. A Roundtable list is created using words that describe a marshmallow provides a useful "bank" of words to draw from while composing the poem.

Roundtable Word Web

Prewriting

This version of Roundtable is for the specific purpose of making a word web. Word webs are usually associated with prewriting. The web begins with a main idea, perhaps "action verbs," or "playing on the teeter-totter." As a paper with the main idea written in the center is circulated around the table, each member of the team adds to the web of ideas.

Simultaneous Roundtable

Prewriting

Every student on the team passes work around the table simultaneously. Student A passes a paper to Student B, B passes to C, and so on.

Each student on the team begins with a paper, so that as papers are passed around the table, each teammate works on one of them. Four ideas can thus circulate simultaneously around a team. For example, a Simultaneous Roundtable on rhyming would include a sheet of paper for each student where rhyming word suggestions are recorded.

Spend-A-Buck

Prewriting

Spend-A-Buck is used to reach consensus or make a decision. Each student is given four "quarters" to spend in any way they wish on the possible choices. All quarters must be spent, but no more than three can be spent by one student on any one choice. The team decision becomes the choice with

the most quarters. Because students must spend on at least two alternatives, a team can make a choice without completely rejecting the ideas not selected at that particular time.

Story Problem Planners

Prewriting

The planners are reproducibles designed to develop the elements of good storytelling.

The classic "good story" has definable characteristics. There must be a hero or heroine with whom the reader identifies. This hero or heroine must face a problem or conflict that stands in the way of achieving something highly desired. The conflict might be another character or a situation. As the main character struggles to achieve his or her goal, greater and greater disasters occur until it seems that success will never come. At the end, the main character's bravery and courage in doing the right thing finally overcome all obstacles, and the story is resolved.

A number of guides are included in the Creating Fiction lesson design to help students outline the elements of a story during prewriting.

Team Brainstorming

Prewriting

Classic brainstorming done simultaneously by small groups is Team Brainstorming.

Brainstorming is a way of opening the floodgates for the release of many ideas, possibilities, concepts, phrases, details, solutions, or suggestions. It is uncensored, unevaluated, synergistic creativity. Kagan uses roles during Brainstorming. One student, the Speed Captain, is in charge of pushing for more output, more responses. The Super Supporter role encourages all ideas, reminding teammates to suspend judgment on everything until later. The Synergy Guru encourages teammates to

build on the ideas of others. The Chief of Silly works to get those crazy ideas from the fringes that so often hold the key to a problem. A Recorder is also a useful role to assign. Using individual sheets of paper to record each idea can also be useful, especially if the teacher wants ideas to be categorized or sorted following the Brainstorming.

Team Collaboration

Writing, Conferring/ Rewriting

Some types of writing are an act of collaboration, with two or more authors working together to create a single piece of writing. An example of this would be a team working together to write a skit in which everyone would play a part. Social skills become crucial in this type of work. Students must discuss and create positive gambits for politely disagreeing, for making suggestions, and for resolving conflicts. In a collaboration, roles and tasks can be assigned based on what needs the teacher perceives in the team or on the skills and talents of the students.

Team Confer

Conferring/Rewriting

Conferring with teammates on questions of content or mechanics is a basic activity in the writing process. As a unit, the team members know each other well. They understand each other's strengths and weaknesses. They have practiced working on social skills together. The writer's team is a critique group and a support group throughout the writing process.

Team Discussion

Prewriting

As a prewriting activity, Team Discussions focus on specific teacher directed questions. "What have we learned about the parts of a letter? Talk it over with your teammates." Team Discussions can also direct students' thinking into creative areas. "What are some of the important issues in our school about which you might write an editorial? Share ideas with your teammates." Team Discussion functions as the anticipatory set in a prewriting activity. Students explore what they already know and anticipate what they would like to write and learn.

Team Interview

Prewriting, Conferring/ Rewriting

In a Team Interview, each member of the team stands in turn and is interviewed by teammates. There is usually a strict time limit set by the teacher for each interview. An example of a timed Team Interview

would be to use it for book reports. If each student had two minutes for the book report, everyone in the class would have delivered an oral book report within eight minutes. Team Interview might be used in conferring on content. Time limits would be more flexible in that case, as students stood to read their stories and be interviewed on questions of content.

Team Performance

Publishing

A choral reading, a puppet show, a skit, a play, a poetry reading, a group investigation project report--all these activities require a team performance. Team Performances can be informal or ceremonial. Teams can perform as a normal part of the classroom routine, or during a special event for parents or other guests.

Team Poem

Team poems are collaborations. Certain criteria might be set for the poem. Perhaps you want a poem written with nothing but prepositions, or a team limerick, or a team poem about the bagpipe player who just performed in the multi-purpose room. After the poems are written, share them in a team display such as Rotating Feedback.

Team Posters

Publishing

When students have worked with only their own teammates during a writing project, Team Posters are an effective way of sharing and publishing the results of the writing. Team Posters include the writing of the team members, possibly art work, illustrations, photographs, colorful labels, and team names. The Team Posters can be displayed in the halls or the classroom.

Team Rehearsal

Conferring

Team Rehearsal is a time for practicing for learning demonstrations, plays, or skits. It gives students an opportunity to polish a performance.

Teams Consult

Conferring/Rewriting

Teams Consult is an entire team consulting with another team.

When teams work to generate ideas or write a group work, they can confer with another team to compare and evaluate the thinking and writing they have completed. For example, if each team has composed paragraphs comparing and contrasting oranges and apples, Teams Consult allows them to confer with another team on clarity, meaning, concepts, comparisons, and other questions of content.

Think-Pair-Share

Prewriting

In Think-Pair-Share, students use an allotted think-time to formulate their ideas on a particular question. Students then pair up and discuss their thoughts with another student. The third step provides the opportunity for students to share their ideas--or their partner's ideas--with the class. Used in prewriting, Think-Pair-Share gives every student a few moments to think and talk about the ideas to be used in the writing assignment.

Think-Pair-Share is uncomplicated but extremely powerful. If teachers used only one technique for prewriting, I would suggest Think-Pair-Share. Here are a few examples. To use Think-Pair-Share in personal narrative, the teacher says, "Think about a time when you were very happy." After a brief think time, the teacher says, "Pair up and talk about your happy time." Let one or two children share with the class. Then tell the children, "Think about the people you were with during your happy time. Think about what they did and what they said. Think about what you said." Again let the children pair up to talk about their ideas, and invite a few to share with the class. Now say, "Think about the place where you were during your happy time. What did you see? What colors did you see? What could you hear or feel or taste? If you were with other people, what did their faces look like?" Repeat the pair discussion and the sharing time. The children will be ready to write a detailed narrative about a happy time in their lives. With slight changes, you can direct the kids thinking to scary times, worried times, proud moments, sad moments, loving moments, angry times, and more.

How about in creating fiction? Tell the students, "Think about a problem a boy or girl might be facing at school or on the way to school." Give think time, then say, "Pair up and talk about what you think the problem could be." Allow several students to contribute ideas during share time. Say, "We have heard about several problems. Think about one you might like to write about. Think about the character having the problem. Is it a boy or a girl? What is the person's name? What grade is he or she in?" Again pair up to discuss ideas, and share a few with the entire class. Say, "What kind of person is your character? Brave? Frightened? Determined? Smart? Does your character have any qualities that might help solve the problem?" Let the students think, pair up to talk out their thoughts, and share with the group. Say, "Think about other kids or grown-ups you might need in your story. Who are they? Give them names. Do they help solve the problem, or are they a part of the problem?" After the Pair and Share steps, ask, "How does your character solve his or her problem?" Pair and Share, continuing with the process if more detail is needed.

Think time can be useful in evoking detail for any writing assignment, from research to book reports. Organize a Corners activity and tell students to pair up for Think-Pair-Share in the Corners. Use Mix-Freeze-Group to pair up for Think-Pair-Share. Use Inside-Outside Circle to form pairs for Think-Pair-Share.

Square

Think-Pair-Square

Prewriting

Think-Pair-Square involves every student in sharing, rather than a few, as in Think-Pair-Share. Pairs square off, forming sets of four. Each student shares first as one of a duo, then as one of a quartet. Paraphrasing is a variation during the "square" step.

The teacher poses a situation. "Imagine you are on a raft floating down a river." Think time is allowed. The teacher says, "Pair up and tell each other what you saw, heard, and felt on your raft." After each member of the pair speaks, pairs share with the other pair on the team.

Think-Write-Pair-Compare

Prewriting

A variation of Think-Pair-Share, this structure puts a writing step between the think time and the pairing up to compare ideas. With little ones, the Write step might be only a word or two. With older students, the Write step could include quick notes or paragraphs. Student pairs could compare written ideas for outlines, formats and notes.

In the chapter The Writing Process and Cooperative Learning, the reader will find a discussion of the relationship between writing and thinking. It will suffice to say that inserting the Write step into the Think-Pair-Share structure to create Think-Write-Pair-Share or Think-Write-Pair-Compare adds enormously to the value of the structure. The act of writing down the ideas from Think time changes and deepens the student's thinking. Nebulous notions clarify when written. Sketchy thinking expands when written. Metaphors emerge. Concepts connect. Then, when students pair up to compare ideas, they have more to offer each other than unrefined thoughts.

Think-Write-Pair-Share

Prewriting

Another variation of Think-Pair-Share, this structure adds a written step between Think time and Pair work.

Word Webbing

Prewriting

Word webbing, or any similar type of semantic mapping, is a versatile and valuable prewriting activity. Students appreciate the freedom of wandering all over a page with lines and circles in a seemingly unruly fashion while generating ideas, plots, and details.

In a word web, the student begins with a main idea or a topic encircled in the center of a paper. Adding to that idea with lines and

Virginia DeBolt: *Write! Cooperative Learning and the Writing Process*

52 Kagan Cooperative Learning • 1 (800) WEE CO-OP

circled words or phrases, the writer creates a web of words related to the main idea. The words and ideas in the word web become the basis for the writing of a first draft. Students can create individual or group word webs.

Write-What-I-Act

Prewriting

Students form pairs. One child acts out a sequential scene, for example, making toast, while the other writes down the steps in order. An opposite structure, Act-What-I-Write, would have students write sequential directions for a partner to attempt to act out.

Reference

Kagan, Spencer. *Cooperative Learning.* San Juan Capistrano, CA, Kagan Cooperative Learning, 1993.

Author Award

In recognition of outstanding achievement in writing

is presented to

_____

this award for _____

_____

Signed _____

Date _____

Virginia DeBolt: *Write! Cooperative Learning and the Writing Process*

Kagan Cooperative Learning • 1 (800) WEE CO-OP

54

Creating Fiction

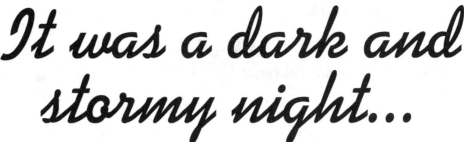

Chapter
6

It was a dark and stormy night...

Lesson-at-a-Glance

Grades	Academic Skills	Time
3 - 6	Using the range of story elements in several different genres.	1-5 sessions

Materials	
• Basic writing materials	• Book binding materials
• Copies of Reproducibles	• Supplies for illustrating stories

Strand

Personal and Imaginitive Writing

Lesson Overview

In this lesson, the student will write a fictional story. Word webbing and planning before beginning to write will help the student create plots, characters, and settings. Using a reproducible, the student will learn to offer positive suggestions as he or she works in revision groups.

Fiction is fun. You will find lots of lesson variations so your students can enjoy writing fiction.

On the one hand... The art of fiction is complex. We speak of plot, characterization, conflict resolution, dialogue, scene and sequel. The world's greatest writers of fiction may spend years learning and perfecting their craft.

On the other hand... Even 4-year olds have an inherent "sense of story." If a story is incomplete, unresolved, or unsatisfying in any way, they demand satisfaction. "What about...?" "What happened to...?" "Why did..."

Children can and will write great fiction. Giving them plenty of classroom time for peer conferencing on content is your greatest contribution as teacher.

Another part of the teacher's role is to point out or let students discover the elements of a good story as the class shares books or videos. Take a few moments after reading a story to reflect on the way in which the author created a character we care about, or gave the character a problem we want to see solved. Talk with the children about the many obstacles the hero or heroine had to overcome, or about how the readers didn't know until the very last how the story would be resolved. Help them analyze such

Structures

- *Corners*
- *Descriptive Spider*
- *Experts Edit*
- *Independent Writing*
- *Inside-Outside Circle*
- *One Stray*
- *Pairs Confer*
- *Story Problem Planners*
- *Team Interview*
- *Word-Webbing*

favorites as *The Little Mermaid* or *A Wrinkle in Time* for their story elements.

When related lessons on topics such as action verbs or quotation marks appear in the course of the year, be sure to tie them to their use in story writing.

Lesson Sequence

Prewrite

Plan a story using
Word Webbing

Have students individually plan a story using the word web reproducible, page 66.

Give writers "What if..." prompts to generate ideas for the word web. Examples of prompts: "What if the beast in *Beauty and the Beast* were female? What if you were ruler of all the playground? What if you woke up one morning to discover you were a dolphin? What would you say to human beings if you were a river? What if you had just one day to save your favorite tree (rock, playground, city) from destruction?"

After brief Think time, say, "Now use the Word Web to help plan the story you will write." In addition to individual word webs, students can make pair or team word webs.

Write

Write a fictional story using
Independent Writing

Each writer will work independently on his or her story. Allow the writer to select the genre most suitable for the story he or she has to tell. Encourage young writers to experiment with new genres. Could the youngster who always tells sports stories give mystery writing a try? Or could the child who likes to write fairy tales give historical fiction a go? In stretching beyond

their usual style, children may find that their writing ability grows with the change.

Confer

The Story Reflections reproducible (page 62) could be used during the feedback process for any of the conferring/rewriting options suggested here.

Confer on content using
Pairs Confer

In pairs, or combined groups of pairs, have students read stories aloud. Focused on content, students discuss how well the story works.

Proof/Edit

Editing Conference using
One Stray

This is a super way to get "fresh eyes" for editing. Although it might sound that way, fresh eyes are not something you get shipped in dry ice. Fresh eyes belong to an editor who isn't already familiar with a story's content.

Students use carbon paper or the photocopier to produce three copies of their revised first draft. They then roam the room for editing conferences with others outside their own team. The one's roam a specified number of teams away from "home." When they return the two's go roaming. Continue until every student has received editing help.

Publish

Celebrate authors using
Anthology

Every six weeks, have each student select his or her best fictional writing from that grading period. Bind it into book form. Have a celebration and let students read

Virginia DeBolt: *Write! Cooperative Learning and the Writing Process*

56   Kagan Cooperative Learning • 1 (800) WEE CO-OP

each other's stories. Collecting authors' autographs for each story in the anthology is fun.

Alternative Activities

Prewrite

Plan a story using
Descriptive Spiders

Using the story planner reproducible, page 60, have students generate ideas to help them when writing descriptive stories.

If students need sensory detail, say, "Write the five senses inside the spider's body. Now label as many legs as you can with information about what you could sense in your story's setting." To develop characterization, say, "Put the names of your important story characters inside the spiders' bodies. Now add as many legs as you can with words describing your character's looks or traits." If students are plagued with passive verbs, say, "Put your overworked verbs, such as 'went, go, said, walk, ran,' inside the spiders' bodies. Now add as many legs as you can naming vivid action verbs." Use these versatile spiders for synonym production, colorful adjective collecting, and more.

Plan a story using
Story Problem Planners

Using one of the story problem planners, pages 63-65, have students develop ideas for a story. The planners might be used in Pair or Team Discussions to help students talk through their ideas for a piece of fiction writing.

Or, before you use one of the planners for the students' stories, you might ask students to use Think-Write-Pair-Share to complete a planner about a book or movie

they are familiar with. In Share time, students learn to identify the elements of story.

Connect writing and literature by encouraging students to borrow a favorite character from a book and plan a new story for that character. They will already have setting and character, and can concentrate on finding a new problem or situation for the character. Have pairs or small groups familiar with the same characters discuss ideas for a story plan. When the stories are finished, compare them with the tone, point of view, and voice found in the original books.

Plan a story using
Inside-Outside Circle

Have the students form two concentric circles. Each student on the inside circle stands facing another student in the outside circle. Give a story prompt, e.g., "Write a story about two people lost in the jungle with only a knife, a box of matches, and a flashlight. Be sure they survive." Have the students discuss ideas to develop characters and plot events.

The writers might carry one of the story planner reproducibles with them to Inside-Outside Circle.

Discuss story openers using
Corners

The teacher picks four story openers from the Story Beginners on pages 67-68. Number them. Write one beginning on each of four large sheets of paper. Tape one up in each corner of the room. Say, "Read these first lines to yourself. Decide which one you think is most interesting, which is a book you'd like to read. Now write the number you picked on a slip of paper. Go to the corner you selected." When students are in corners, say, "Pair up and talk about why you liked the story beginning you picked." After the children have shared, say, "Form groups of four. Be ready to share two reasons why the beginning you picked is a good one." Students from each of the corners share the qualities that make their choice a good story beginning. Tell the students to return to their desks. Follow with a brief Class Discussion summarizing what students just learned about the characteristics of a good story beginning.

Teachers might want to repeat this Corners activity periodically during the year. If the kids are willing, you could put their (anonymous) story beginnings in the corners.

Confer

Confer on content with older students using *Corners*

Invite in four students from a grade level above that of your students. Choose positive-minded critiquers who understand the elements of good stories. Older students, as expert tutors, help students by listening to their stories and making positive suggestions about content. Send writers to the experts in pairs or triads and you will get the free-for-nothing bonus of peer conferencing, too.

Confer on content using *Team Interview*

Each team member stands in turn and reads his or her story aloud. Teammates then interview the author. Questions unanswered in the story make good interview questions. Knowing more about what listeners wanted to hear gives the writer an instant revision plan.

After any type of conference on story content, allow time for students to work on revisions and changes.

Proof/Edit

Editing Conference using *Pairs Confer*

Working in pairs, children help each other with proofreading and editing.

Editing Conference with older children using *Corners*

Invite students from grades above that of your students. Set them up in Corners to provide expert editing and proofreading help.

Editing Conference using *Experts Edit*

Choose four or eight students from your class who are experts at spelling and mechanics and arrange for them to help the other students with editing.

Publish

Celebrate authors using *Authors Party*

Caldicott, Newbery and Pulitzer, here we come! Have a party with celebrations, congratulations, awards, and refreshments. Let authors share their stories with the class.

Celebrate authors using *Read In*

In a whole class Roundtable, pass the students' stories and books from kid to kid so that everyone has the opportunity to read the pieces written by classmates. Attach blank sheets to the work with a paper clip so that readers can make positive comments for the author. Reading all afternoon or all

Virginia DeBolt: *Write! Cooperative Learning and the Writing Process*

58   Kagan Cooperative Learning • 1 (800) WEE CO-OP

day is lots of fun, especially if you have pillows, cushions, sleeping bags, food, and even get to take off your shoes.

Create class or school library books using *Book It*

Collect stories from the class and bind them into a book or a literary magazine to place in the classroom or the school library. Why not publish a literary journal every six weeks?

References

Graves, Donald H. *Experiment with Fiction.* Heinemann, Portsmouth, NH: 1989.

Graves' little book is packed with action ideas for helping children with leads, characters, plots, and endings. It details the type of fiction children are likely to create at various stages of development.

Descriptive Spiders

Name _____

Directions: Add words at the ends of the spider's legs to help you describe the characters in your story.

Types of Fiction I Have Written

Name_____

Genre	**Titles**

Talking Animals_____

Fairy Tales_____

Overcoming Great Odds_____

Contemporary_____

Historical_____

Personal Experience_____

Animal Story_____

Sports Story_____

True-Life Adventure_____

Romance_____

Science Fiction_____

Fantasy_____

Suspense_____

Mystery_____

Other_____

_____

Story Reflections

Author_____

Story Title_____

Helper_____

Comments on the setting:

Comments on the characters:

Comments on the plot (story problems and solutions):

Strongest points:

Questions I'd like answered:

Other comments:

Virginia DeBolt: *Write! Cooperative Learning and the Writing Process*
Kagan Cooperative Learning • 1 (800) WEE CO-OP

62

Story Planner

Name _____

Title

Main Character

Setting

Problem

Solution

Story Planner

Title_____

Author_____

Setting

Time and place of the story are_____

Character

The main character_____has these

traits_____

Goal

The main character really wants to_____

_____

Problem

However,_____

_____

Events Leading to Solution

So,_____

_____

_____

Ending

The character finally_____

_____

Virginia DeBolt: *Write! Cooperative Learning and the Writing Process*

64   Kagan Cooperative Learning • 1 (800) WEE CO-OP

Story Planner

Name _____

Directions: Sometimes the main character in a story has to achieve several small goals to reach his or her main goal. Use this chart to plan problems and solutions leading to the final resolution of your story.

Character's Main Goal

Problem and Solution

Problem and Solution

Problem and Solution

Final Outcome

Word Web

Name _____

Directions: Use a word web to plan ideas for characters and events in your story. As you think of more ideas, add more ovals and lines to the web.

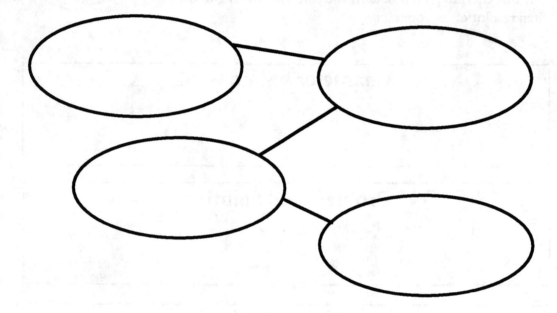

Virginia DeBolt: *Write! Cooperative Learning and the Writing Process*
Kagan Cooperative Learning • 1 (800) WEE CO-OP

Story Beginners for Corners Activity

My father is always talking about how a dog can be very educational for a boy. This is one reason I got a cat.
It's Like This, Cat **by Emily Neville**

It was a dark and stormy night.
A Wrinkle in Time
by Madeleine L'Engle

The sun did not shine.
It was too wet to play.
So we sat in the house
All that cold, cold, wet day.
The Cat in the Hat
by Dr. Seuss

Life was going along okay when my mother and father dropped the news. Bam! Just like that.
Superfudge **by Judy Blume**

All children, except one, grow up.
Peter Pan **by J.M. Barrie**

The summer that Arthur Rasby was ten years old was a problem summer.
Arthur, For the Very First Time
by Patricia MacLachlan

Chug, chug, chug. Puff, puff, puff.
Ding-dong, ding-dong.
The Little Engine that Could
by Watty Piper

The Herdmans were absolutely the worst kids in the history of the world. They lied and stole and smoked cigars (even the girls) and talked dirty and hit little kids and cussed their teachers and took the name of the Lord in vain and set fire to Fred Shoemaker's old broken down toolhouse.
The Best Christmas Pageant Ever
by Barbara Robinson

Story Beginners for Corners Activity

When Mary Lennox was sent to Misselthwaite Manor to live with her uncle, everybody said she was the most disagreeable-looking child ever seen. It was true, too.
The Secret Garden
by Frances Hodgson Burnett

The small brown mouse named Ralph who was hiding under the grandfather clock did not have much longer to wait before he could ride his motorcycle.
Runaway Ralph
by Beverly Cleary

This morning I wanted to make breakfast just for you...but the eggs were too slippery.
Just For You **by Mercer Mayer**

One day Petey, who was a puppy, said to his mother, who was a dog, "I'd like a boy for Christmas."
The Puppy Who Wanted a Boy
by Jane Thayer

It was not that Omri didn't appreciate Patrick's birthday present to him. Far from it. He was really very grateful--sort of.
The Indian in the Cupboard
by Lynne Reid Banks

Mr. and Mrs. Mallard were looking for a place to live. But every time Mr. Mallard saw what looked like a nice place, Mrs. Mallard said it was no good.
Make Way for Ducklings
by Robert McCloskey

Lewis skidded down the stairs and into the living room. "I can't take a bath," he announced. "There's a Beast in the bathtub."
The Beast in the Bathtub
by Kathleen Stevens

The night Max wore his wolf suit and made mischief of one kind and another his mother called him "WILD THING."
Where the Wild Things Are
by Maurice Sendak

Samplings

"The Frog that croak his last croak

One sunny afternoon in the swamps there lived a sick frog. He had a sore croaker. He layed in bed and watched tv. He played chess with his shawdow. He decided to fix him a bowl of says with a fly...

Adrian Garcia
Gr. 5 Hillcrest School
Carlsbad, NM

Television

Cristal Briggs
1-23-92

I was watching my favorite tv show. the ahowoncer says come on and join us. I steped into the screen.

I started playing the show. I won the contest and became a star and when I was Pinished there was no why out unless some one came by and turned the tv off...

Cristal Briggs
Gr. 4 Hillcrest School
Carlsbad, NM

Samplings

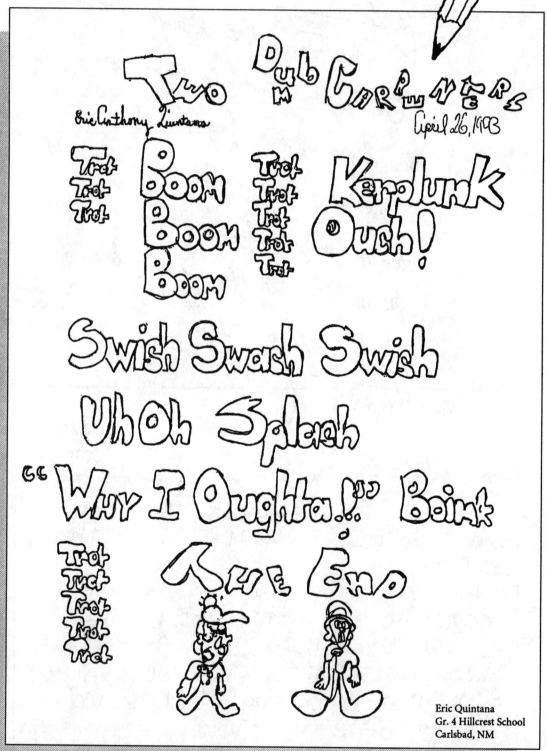

Eric Quintana
Gr. 4 Hillcrest School
Carlsbad, NM

Virginia DeBolt: *Write! Cooperative Learning and the Writing Process*
Kagan Cooperative Learning • 1 (800) WEE CO-OP

Creating Fiction

Peer Response	Title _____
	Name _____

_____

_____

_____

_____

_____

_____

_____

_____

_____

_____

_____

_____

_____

_____

_____

_____

_____

_____

_____

_____

_____

_____

_____

_____

_____

Gambits:

1. The most vivid part was

_____

_____.

2. Could you tell me more

about _____

_____

_____?

Virginia DeBolt: *Write! Cooperative Learning and the Writing Process*

Kagan Cooperative Learning • 1 (800) WEE CO-OP   71

Plays and Skits

Break a Leg

Lesson-at-a-Glance

Grades	Academic Skills	Time
3 - 6	• Scriptwriting • Set design • Performing	One week to a month

Materials	Strand
• Basic writing materials • Other materials determined by students	Personal and Imaginative Writing

Lesson Overview

In this lesson, the students will write team plays and perform them for classmates. During prewriting, students will role play and act out their ideas, so that they have a sense of what they want to do before they begin writing. Students will accomplish the numerous details involved in writing and performing a play by dividing the tasks among teammates.

Kids are the writers, directors, stagehands and stars, but the teacher is always the producer.

Since putting on a play may involve many tasks, establish teams with care. The team doing a puppet play as a book report may be quite different from the team doing a staged production for parents.

- **Jigsaw**
- **Roundtable**
- **Team Collaboration**
- **Teams Confer**
- **Team Discussion**
- **Team Performance**
- **Team Rehearsal**

Structures

Lesson Sequence

Prewrite
Develop ideas for a play using
Team Discussion

During the initial team discussion students work out an idea for the play. A Recorder notes group suggestions for characters, plots, and other ideas. Tell them, "Role play some of the characters and situations you have planned. Don't write down a script yet. First act out parts of it to see how it looks and sounds." Allow ample time for this discussion and role playing. Then say, "When you're ready, work together to write a script."

Write
Teams write plays using
Team Collaboration

Teammates work on the first draft of the play. The use of roles such as Recorder, Taskmaster, Gatekeeper, and Encourager often prove very helpful in the smooth functioning of the group during the writing of the first draft.

Confer

Confer on content using
Teams Confer

If the team collaboration on script writing has gone well, teams may not require much revising and editing. However, if they do, scriptwriters from different teams set up writing conferences to assist each other with the plays. Any changes or revisions are made following this conference.

Proof/Edit

Editing Conference using
Roundtable

Scriptwriters meet again to examine scripts for mechanics. This group should meet with the teacher to study plays in books to see how they are formatted and punctuated. Writers prepare the final draft following this conference. Have photocopies made for all team members. If the play will be published as a performance, there is no need to edit or proofread.

Practice the play using *Team Rehearsal*

Teams need several rehearsals before their actual performance. By this point in the process, teams have a very clear idea of what they are doing, and need help from you only with the last few (!) details.

Publish

Give the play using
Team Performance

Teams perform the plays before their classmates and/or other audiences.

Alternative Activities

Proof/Edit

Teammates specialize using
Jigsaw

When the creation of a concept and a first draft are complete, the teacher may opt to move into the Jigsaw structure. The decision to split the teams for Jigsaw will be based on the complexity of the play or skit the class is planning.

Once the script of the play is written, the team can divide up tasks. Each person will carry out one aspect of the play's production, contributing to the overall team effort. Teams may need a director, stage hands, costumers, actors, puppet makers, musicians, artists for posters and programs, or other workers. Every team member is an actor and has other tasks as well. Teams have a conference every day to discuss needs and manage problems. The Taskmaster is responsible for checking on progress each day, and keeping the team informed about how preparations are going. The teacher, as

---

- The work involved in writing, producing, and performing uses every learning modality
- Dramatizing a story
- Performing folktales for younger students
- Book reports
- Puppet shows
- Culminating a research project
- Demonstrating learning
- Program for parents
- D.A.R.E. graduation program
- Just for fun

A few reasons to write and perform plays

Virginia DeBolt: *Write! Cooperative Learning and the Writing Process*

74   Kagan Cooperative Learning • 1 (800) WEE CO-OP

producer, sets up deadlines and facilitates scheduling. A Resource Manager is responsible for working with the teacher to coordinate such activities as securing the school's puppet stage, arranging sound or music equipment.

An important part of this very active process is for individuals to devote 10 minutes each day to writing in the Learner's Journal. Writers reflect on how the group is working, how they are coming with deadlines, new skills they are learning, and plan the next day's work.

Helpful Books for Teacher

Young, John Wray and Margaret Mary. *How to Produce the Play: the complete production handbook.* Chicago: The Dramatic Publishing Company, 1977. My friend the drama teacher says she's worn out three of these from frequent use.

Spolin, Viola. *Improvisation for the Theater.* Evanston, Illinois: Northwestern University Press, 1983. This book devotes a special section to children and the theater. Spolin has other books on the subject, including *Theater Games for the Classroom: A Teacher's Handbook.*

Virginia DeBolt: *Write! Cooperative Learning and the Writing Process*

Kagan Cooperative Learning • 1 (800) WEE CO-OP   75

Samplings

THE BLONDE BABES

Carolyn: "Look at those good looking guys!"

Claudine: "The blond one's kind of cute."

Rose: "Which one? There's two!"

Rosalyn: "I kind of think there both ugly. I like the one
            with the brownish goldish hair. He's a hunk!"

Claudine: "You like him, disgusting."

Rose: "Well, I sort of like him to."

Rosalyn: "But I saw him first!"

Carolyn: "Cut it out you two."

Rosalyn: "He's still mine. Oh, look he's got a twin coming
            out of the bathroom."

Rose: "Well I didn't like him anyway."

Claudine: "Carolyn, which one do you like?"

Carolyn: "I like the one with blond hair."

Rosalyn: "I've got to get him to notice me. Any ideas?"

Rose: "Do you want to play frisbee to show him how
            athletic you are?"

Rosalyn: "That's a great idea. Come on, lets go."…

A five page play by the team The Blonde Babes:
Amanda Brantley, Michelle Goeke, Stacy Snow, Lisa Sullivan,
Gr. 5 Hillcrest School
Carlsbad, NM

Virginia DeBolt: *Write! Cooperative Learning and the Writing Process*

Kagan Cooperative Learning • 1 (800) WEE CO-OP

76

Plays & Skits

Peer Response

Title _____

Name _____

_____

_____

_____

_____

_____

_____

_____

_____

_____

_____

_____

_____

_____

_____

_____

_____

_____

_____

_____

_____

_____

_____

_____

_____

_____

Gambits:

1. I enjoyed the _____
character because _____
_____.

2. It was helpful to me when
_____
_____
_____.

Virginia DeBolt: *Write! Cooperative Learning and the Writing Process*
Kagan Cooperative Learning • 1 (800) WEE CO-OP

77

Poetry

Roses are Red

Lesson-at-a-Glance

Grades	Academic Skills	Time
3 - 6	Writing Poetry	1 or 2 sessions

Materials		Strand
• Basic writing materials	• A motivating "object"	Personal and Imaginative Writing
• Cubing reproducible	• Refreshments for	
• Scissors & glue	Poetry Reading	

Lesson Overview

For poets to thrive, prewriting poetry is a year-long attitude in the classroom. That attitude reflects love of words: the sounds and rhythms of words, the look of words, the discovery of meaningful new words. Use a bulletin board called Wonderful Words, a learning center called Wordsmiths' Corner, or a snake whose coiled form grows along the wall as words are added during the year…attention paid to words nurtures the young poet.

The teacher nurtures poetry by seizing moments of wonder, curiosity, or emotion which occur through the year. Did someone bring a rabbit to class? Write a poem. Were the trees covered with frost this morning? There's a poem. Did the class earn a bubble gum reward? Thirty bubble blowers each make a poem. I tend to write poems on the board in the midst of things. I'll see a kid do something funny or beautiful and I'll make a poem out of it, right then and there. Modeling does matter.

Lesson Sequence

Prewrite

Examine an object using *Cube-It Brainstorming*

When cubing, students look at a something from six different sides (see cube reproducible, page 83). Pass out the cube pattern and have each student cut and glue it. The teacher brings an object — an orange, a toy, an Indian headdress, a piece of music — and shows it to the class. Using the cube, each student spends three to five minutes individually brainstorming ideas and words related to the object.

Structures

- • *Cube-It Brainstorming*
- • *Independent Writing*
- • *Numbered Heads Apart*
- • *Roundtable*
- • *Simultaneous Roundtable*
- • *Team Discussion*

Write

Write a poem using
Independent Writing

Children work independently on their poems. I remind them: poems do not have to rhyme.

Confer

Confer on content using
Numbered Heads Apart

Establish writing conference circles in the four corners of the room. All team members numbered one meet in one corner, the two's in another corner, and so on. In the corners, kids group themselves into conference circles of 4 or 5 students. Students bring to the conference their poems, a pencil, and something hard to write on. Each child reads his or her poem in the conference circle. Students help each other with words, rhymes, clarity, and other aspects of each poem. Everyone then returns to their desks for rewriting.

Proof/Edit

Editing Conference using
Roundtable

In teams, students pass the revised poems around for editing and proofreading. Each paper will be checked by three children before it returns to its owner. Students then prepare a clean final copy.

Publish

Share poems using
Poetry Reading

Have the poets read the poems aloud during a special celebration. Invite guests, serve punch and cookies, and honor the poets and their poems.

Alternative Activities

Prewrite

Share impressions using
Team Discussion

Within teams, students share ideas and impressions about an object provided by the teacher. During the Team Discussion, students add to or refine their ideas. Allow three to five minutes for discussion.

Rhymin' Simon using
Simultaneous Roundtable

Each student writes key words or phrases from a poem he or she wants to write. The sheets are passed round the table so that teammates write rhyming words on each paper in turn. Each sheet of paper might make two or three rounds of the table to provide each author with a handy, helpful supply of rhyming words.

Lesson Extension

Adjective Expression using
Team Poem

Tell the students that they are going outside as a team to observe a tree. Tell them each team can pick any tree within a specified area. Then say, "If you are a One, you will lie on your back on the ground directly under the tree and look up toward the sky through the tree. Two's will stand very close to the trunk and look at the trunk. Three's will stand near a branch and look at the leaves. Four's will stand back at least 50 feet away from the tree. Write down every adjective you can think of to describe what you see."

Virginia DeBolt: *Write! Cooperative Learning and the Writing Process*

80   Kagan Cooperative Learning • 1 (800) WEE CO-OP

Bring the teams back into the classroom. Say, "Your team will work together on a poem describing your tree. There's one special rule for your poem. Every word in the poem must be an adjective." When the teams are finished, invite them to share their poems with the class.

Another Poetry Possibility
A Bio-Poem

I would like to give credit to the originator of the Bio-Poem, but, alas, I have seen it printed and used in many contexts without attribution. Perhaps someone out there knows. Please share that knowledge with me. A reproducible is provided on page 82.

Bio-Poem

Line 1:   Your first name only
Line 2:   Four traits that describe you
Line 3:   Sibling of (or son of, mother of, teacher of)
Line 4:   Lover of (three people or ideas)
Line 5:   Who feels (three responses)
Line 6:   Who needs (three responses)
Line 7:   Who gives (three responses)
Line 8:   Who fears (three responses)
Line 9:   Who would like to see (three responses)
Line 10: Who lives at/in
Line 11: Your last name only

BIO Poem

Gretel

1.	First name	Gretel
2.	Four traits	Small, lost, tired, hungry
3.	Related to	Sister of Hansel
4.	Cares deeply about	Cares deeply about her family
5.	Who feels	Who feels afraid
6.	Who needs	Who needs a place to sleep
7.	Who gives	Who gives companionship
8.	Who fears	Who fears the witch
9.	Who would like to see	Who would like to see her father again
10.	Resident of	Resident of the forest
11.	Last Name	

Your turn: Write a BIO poem about yourself.

1. _____

2. _____, _____, _____, _____

3. _____

4. Cares deeply about _____

5. Who feels _____

6. Who needs _____

7. Who gives _____

8. Who fears _____

9. Who would like _____

10. Resident of _____

11. _____

Virginia DeBolt: *Write! Cooperative Learning and the Writing Process*
Kagan Cooperative Learning • 1 (800) WEE CO-OP

82

Poetry Cubing

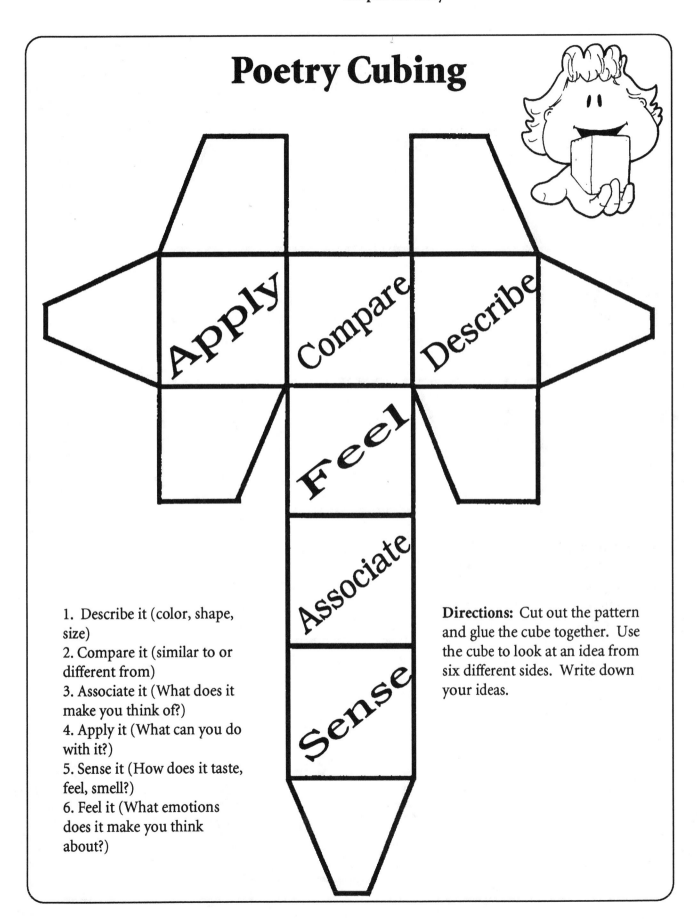

Apply

Compare

Describe

Feel

Associate

Sense

1. Describe it (color, shape, size)

2. Compare it (similar to or different from)

3. Associate it (What does it make you think of?)

4. Apply it (What can you do with it?)

5. Sense it (How does it taste, feel, smell?)

6. Feel it (What emotions does it make you think about?)

Directions: Cut out the pattern and glue the cube together. Use the cube to look at an idea from six different sides. Write down your ideas.

Virginia DeBolt: *Write! Cooperative Learning and the Writing Process*
Kagan Cooperative Learning • 1 (800) WEE CO-OP

83

Cubing

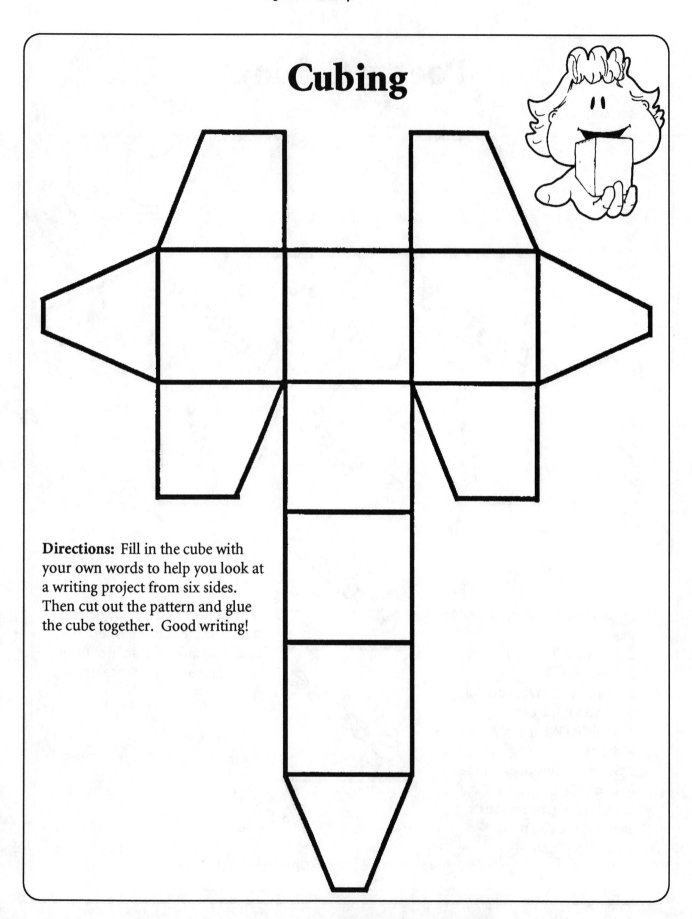

Directions: Fill in the cube with your own words to help you look at a writing project from six sides. Then cut out the pattern and glue the cube together. Good writing!

Virginia DeBolt: *Write! Cooperative Learning and the Writing Process*

Kagan Cooperative Learning • 1 (800) WEE CO-OP

84

Poetry Cubing

Record your ideas here.

_____

_____

_____

_____

_____

_____

_____

_____

_____

_____

_____

_____

_____

_____

_____

_____

_____

_____

_____

_____

_____

Virginia DeBolt: *Write! Cooperative Learning and the Writing Process*
Kagan Cooperative Learning • 1 (800) WEE CO-OP

85

Samplings

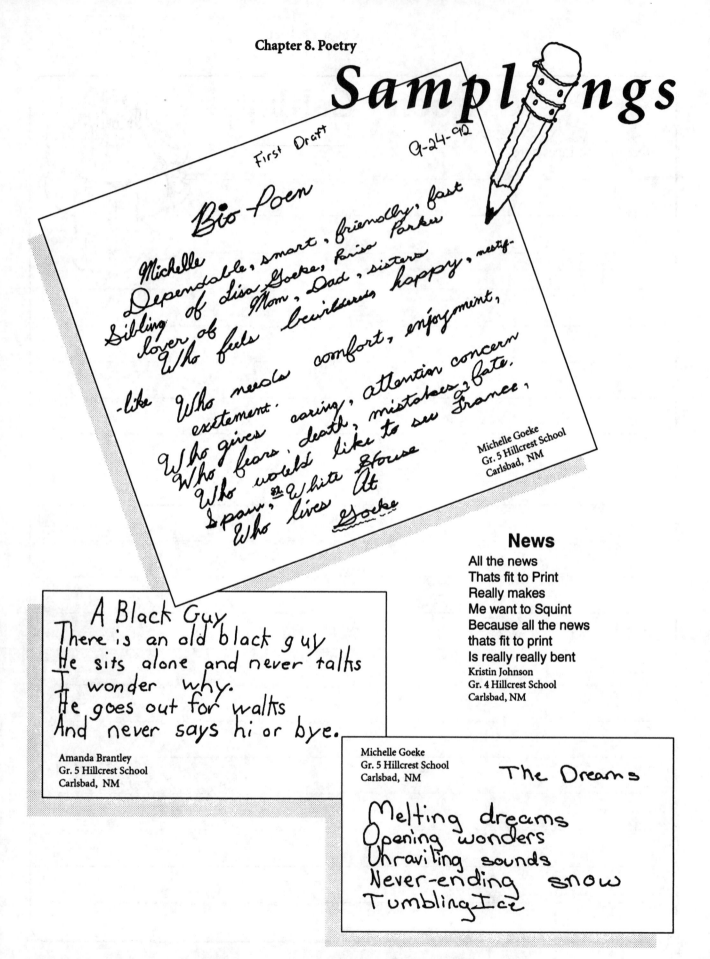

First Draft   9-24-92

Bio Poem

Michelle
Dependable, smart, friendly, fast
Sibling of Lisa Goeke, Krisa Parker
lover of Mom, Dad, sisters
Who feels bewildered, happy, nesty-
-like
Who needs comfort, enjoyment,
excitement.
Who gives caring, attention concern
Who fears death, mistakes, fate.
Who would like to see France,
Spain, White House At
Who lives
            Goeke

Michelle Goeke
Gr. 5 Hillcrest School
Carlsbad, NM

News

All the news
Thats fit to Print
Really makes
Me want to Squint
Because all the news
thats fit to print
Is really really bent

Kristin Johnson
Gr. 4 Hillcrest School
Carlsbad, NM

A Black Guy
There is an old black guy
He sits alone and never talks
I wonder why.
He goes out for walks
And never says hi or bye.

Amanda Brantley
Gr. 5 Hillcrest School
Carlsbad, NM

Michelle Goeke
Gr. 5 Hillcrest School
Carlsbad, NM

The Dreams

Melting dreams
Opening wonders
Unraviling sounds
Never-ending snow
Tumbling Ice

Virginia DeBolt: *Write! Cooperative Learning and the Writing Process*

Poetry

Peer Response

Title _____

Name _____

_____

_____

_____

_____

_____

_____

_____

_____

_____

_____

_____

_____

_____

_____

_____

_____

_____

_____

_____

_____

_____

_____

_____

_____

_____

_____

Gambits:

1. The part of the poem I liked best was _____

_____

_____.

2. The words made me think of _____

_____

_____.

Virginia DeBolt: _Write! Cooperative Learning and the Writing Process_

Kagan Cooperative Learning • 1 (800) WEE CO-OP

Personal Narrative

All About Me...

Lesson-at-a-Glance

Grades	Academic Skills	Time
3 - 6	Writing personal experiences	1-3 periods

Materials	Strand
• Basic writing materials • Reproducible Peer Conference Response Forms	Personal & Imaginative Writing

Lesson Overview

In this lesson, the student will write a narrative about a personal experience or memory. Students will learn ways of selecting topics from the fertile ground of their real life experience.

Personal narrative is, well...personal. Teachers who assign topics for personal writing will receive in return assignments; not writing. Instead of assigning, provide. Provide time regularly during the year for personal narrative writing. Provide choice: choice of topic, choice of genre. Students write more freely, more often, and more fluently on personal topics of their own choosing than on any other type of writing. A warning! Be prepared for the truth, the whole truth, and nothing but the truth when you provide opportunities for personal narratives. As teacher, be ready to respond to the writer as well as the writing.

Sometimes personal narratives are so charged with emotion that a supply of Kleenex is an important tool in your kit of writing supplies.

A valuable prewriting tool for personal narrative writing is the ongoing list attached to the student's writing folder, "Ideas for Writing." See writing folder forms in Chapter 4.

Lesson Sequence

Prewrite Pick a topic using *Card Magic*
Transfer the ideas on the student's writing folder "Ideas to Write About" list to cards. Put one idea on each card. Have the students work in pairs to select five ideas apiece. Designate one student to be student A, the

Structures
- *Card Magic*
- *Team Discussion*
- *Think-Pair-Square*
- *Independent Writing*
- *Numbered Heads Apart*
- *Roundtable Edit*
- *Spend-A-Buck*

other to be student B. Student A gives her five cards to student B, who mixes them up and scatters them face down on the desk. Then Student A holds her hand in the air above the cards until the magic emanations from the cards draw her hand down to the card which will name her writing topic for the day. Student B selects his topic in the same way. If you feel like humming the theme from The Twilight Zone while doing this, it's quite all right.

An alternative to using the prepared list from the writing folder is to hand each child five cards and say, "Brainstorm five ideas that you might be able to write about today. Put one idea on each card." Choose one of the five ideas with help from the card's magic emanations as described above.

Hang on to the unselected cards. They can be used another day.

Write
Write a narrative using
Independent Writing
Students work independently to write a first draft.

Confer
Confer on content using
Numbered Heads Apart
Each child needs a Peer Conference Response Form and his/her rough draft. Students number off within teams. One's from every team meet in a designated area, two's in another, and so on. This creates four groups of students for writing conferences. Within the new groups, have pairs or triads form the response groups. As students read the rough drafts aloud, the listeners complete the Peer Conference Response Forms. A reproducible is provided

in Chapter 3. To emphasize careful listening, the completed response forms could be left face down in the center of the response team until each person has a turn. Students return to their desks to work on needed revisions.

Proof/Edit
Editing Conference using
Roundtable
Students pass revised drafts to each member of their base team for a Roundtable Edit. As teammates pass the pieces around the table, each writer receives three editors help.

Each individual then prepares a polished draft of his or her narrative work.

Publish
All the drafts are placed in the student's writing folder. Other publishing options are a matter of personal choice.

Alternative Activities

Prewrite
Think of a topic using
Think-Pair-Square
Teachers direct students thinking in personal narrative with Think time prompts, such as, "Think about a time you felt happy. Pair up and discuss your ideas...Now square up and discuss happy times with your team." Other prompts could include: "Think about the scariest experience you have ever had. Think about the thing you wish for the most. Think about something funny you have seen happen. Think about all the things you like about school. Think about why you like Nintendo games. Think about the stories your parents tell about what you did as a baby."

Select writing topics using
Team Discussion

Have students discuss their list of writing ideas with teammates. Have team members assist each other in deciding which idea might be most important or interesting to write about at this time.

Select a topic using
Spend-A-Buck

Manipulatives representing quarters are required. Use tokens, play money, jelly beans, chips, M & M's, (etcetera, etcetera, etcetera). Each team member has 4 "quarters." On small slips of paper, each team member records three ideas he or she might like to write about that day. Beginning with teammate #1, and going in turn, each student displays his three topic ideas. Student #1's slips of paper with the ideas on them are placed in the center of the team. Team members indicate which idea sounds most interesting to them, which idea they would most like to hear about, by spending a buck.

In Spend-A-Buck, a student can spend quarters in any way she likes by placing the quarters on the idea of her choice. There are two rules. On each turn, all four quarters have to be spent. You can't put more than three quarters on any one choice.

Each student in turn lays out his ideas. The team puts its money where its mouth is and spends a buck on the most interesting topic. Voila! Everybody has a topic.

Lesson Extension

Personal Artifacts and Classroom Museums

When children bring to the classroom personal items of some significance or importance to them, excellent personal narrative writing can result. The writing could be published by displaying the various items in a classroom museum, with the children's written descriptions as part of the display. Old tools and household gadgets sometimes have incomprehensible uses to our modern technology-smart kids. A museum of such fascinating goodies would merit invitations to other classes for a visit. Your writers, turned museum curators, could then read, describe, display artifacts, and talk about their museum pieces.

Suggestions of interesting personal artifacts for narrative writing include: an object that has been in the family for two or more generations, a favorite toy, a favorite doll, photos or drawings of pets, a souvenir from a place once visited, an object from the student's babyhood, photos of parents and/or grandparents.

Samplings

My Girlfriend

It all started when I was 1 year old. I was on my porch. I saw little girl on her porch. I said "you come over." Everything was going just real fine when my grandma heard her crying.

My grandma went outside because she was crying her head off. I was laughing my head off. My grandma asked me "what did you do to her?" I said "we pull hair me kiss". My grandma got really mad at me. I got a whipping for that. Ever since that my grand pulls my hair for a kiss.

Rudy Richardson
Gr. 4 Hillcrest School
Carlsbad, NM

My Little Brother

Jacob Worth

My little brother is bad news. He's always getting me in trouble. He could get anybody in trouble, even the smartest person in the world. He's what I guess you call a nuisance. One time he cussed me out like a sailor. He said that I cussed him out. I had to wash my mouth out with soap.

There's no telling what he'll do to me today.

Jacob Worth
Gr. 5 Hillcrest School
Carlsbad, NM

Spelling Words

Lisa
2/9/93

In spelling we get to choose our own spelling words. I find weird words from a spelling Bee book. One of the weird words I had last week was aorta. Ms De Bolt thought it was spelled acorta. She always questions these strange words.

Lisa Sullivan
Gr. 5 Hillcrest School
Carlsbad, NM

Virginia DeBolt: *Write! Cooperative Learning and the Writing Process*

Kagan Cooperative Learning • 1 (800) WEE CO-OP

92

Samplings

My Cat

Across the street there was an old man. He was poor. He had a cat. I started to play with it. He had a cat. I started to play with it. He came over and said, "you can have him, because I don't have money to buy him food." I went and asked my mom. She said, "no, I don't think so." I started crying.

Gloria Patterson
Gr. 4 Hillcrest School
Carlsbad, NM

If I could trade places   Stacy

If I could trade places I would trade places with Lisa. Lisa is smart and nice. I think I would be able to understand her better. if I was in her place. I would understand her thoughts, her point of view, and her feelings. I would no why she doesn't like lima beans.

Stacy Snow
Gr. 5 Hillcrest School
Carlsbad, NM

What Where Going to do on Christ

This Christmas all my family is going to South Carolina. Too see my aunt, She sended photo graphes she took, I wish she never did move. Because if my mom coudnt aford some thing expecive, She would bye it, I feel excited to visit har, She sang rock a my baby to my brother, She is the nicest aunt a boy can ever have,

Mauricio Gomez
Gr. 4 Hillcrest School
Carlsbad, NM

Virginia DeBolt: *Write! Cooperative Learning and the Writing Process*
Kagan Cooperative Learning • 1 (800) WEE CO-OP

93

Personal Narrative

Peer Response

Title _____

Name _____

_____

_____

_____

_____

_____

_____

_____

_____

_____

_____

_____

_____

_____

_____

_____

_____

_____

_____

_____

_____

_____

_____

_____

Work in Progress

Gambits:

1. The part I found most interesting was _____

_____

_____ .

2. I'd like to learn more about _____

_____

_____

_____ .

Virginia DeBolt: *Write! Cooperative Learning and the Writing Process*
Kagan Cooperative Learning • 1 (800) WEE CO-OP

A Learner's Journal

Log It!

Lesson-at-a-Glance

Grades	Academic Skills	Time
3 - 6	• Critical thinking • Writing a descriptive paragraph • Applying math skills to solve a problem • Finding area in square yards	1 or 2 math periods

Materials
- Yardsticks
- Rulers
- Tape measures
- Students may invent measuring devices of their own.

Strand
Personal and Imaginative Writing

An old Chinese proverb states, "I hear and I forget; I see and I remember; I write and I understand."

Lesson Overview

In this lesson, the student will use his or her Learning Journal to think/learn his or her way through a problem. As the student tests ideas, he or she will add new insights to the journal. When a satisfactory solution is found, the student will reflect on his or her own learning process.

The Learner's Journal offers an opportunity for students to learn to write and think clearly about any subject. It is fertile ground for metacognition, that is, for students to think about their thinking.

The act of writing about learning will bring two positive results. First, students will improve thinking and learning across the curriculum. Have children write out the steps to long division, write about discoveries made during science activities, write gambit suggestions for writing conferences, write about everything! Research suggests that students who write about what they study improve learning. (Applebee, 1986)

The second result is better writing. To become adequate writers, students need many opportunities to write every day. Thus, a Learner's Journal is a powerful mechanism for teachers who want a practical way to enhance learning and writing.

- *Chalkboard Share*
- *Class Discussion*
- *Independent Writing*
- *Pairs Consult*
- *Pairs Experiment*
- *Team Discussion*

Structures

Virginia DeBolt: *Write! Cooperative Learning and the Writing Process*
Kagan Cooperative Learning • 1 (800) WEE CO-OP

95

Lesson Sequence

Prewrite

Review learning using
Team Discussion

Challenge students with a real problem. "We need to know how many square yards of carpeting it would take to cover our room with carpet." Allow them a brief (two to three minutes) Team Discussion to review math learning that might be useful in solving the problem.

Write

Plan a strategy using
Independent Writing

In their Learner's Journal, students write a step-by-step description of how they would find the number of square yards needed. Encourage students to explain their thinking: Why did they choose a particular method of finding the answer?

Confer

Confer on content using
Pairs Consult

Student pairs read their paragraphs to each other. Discussion should focus on clarity of content and method. If there are gaps in thinking, pairs work together to be sure that each completely understands the other's idea for finding the area. The two do not have to agree on a "correct way" to solve the problem. They do have to understand each other's approach.

Test a strategy using
Pairs Experiment

Working together, the pair moves around the room to carry out the plan in each Learner's Journal. While students mea-sure, the teacher should prepare the chalkboard or overhead projector so answers can be recorded.

Share answers using
Chalkboard Share

When the students find the area, they record the answer in their journal and on the chalkboard or overhead.

Share results using
Class Discussion

When all the pairs are finished, there will be a list of answers for the class to study. If there is disagreement about the correct area, tell students to write in their journals about possible ways to test answers or in-sure accuracy.

Reflect on thinking using
Independent Writing

Students write another paragraph telling what they now know about finding area, problems or successes they had with their method, and ideas for future work in find-ing area.

Publish

A journal is not published as other types of writing are, because it is for personal use, and because Journal writing should not be treated as a polished product. It is a valu-able place for the teacher and the student to conduct a dialog on the student's thinking and learning. Have students hand in the journal for a response from the teacher. A "response" in a Learner's Journal is not grading or correcting. Instead, return it with one pertinent comment or question about the student's learning. Atwell (1987) suggests that the comment should affirm, challenge, or extend the writer's thinking.

Evaluation

Ask students to use self-evaluation in the Learner's Journal. Have them look through the journal for signs of progress in thinking, writing, and learning. Then have them write their self-evaluation in their Learner's Journal.

Lesson Extension

Buddy Journals

After students have written a journal entry, they exchange journals to give each other feedback or affirmation.

References

Applebee, Arthur N., Judith A. Langer, and Ina V. S. Mullis. *The Writing Report Card.* Princeton, New Jersey: Educational Testing Service, 1986.

Atwell, Nancie. *In the Middle: Writing, Reading, and Learning with Adolescents.* Upper Montclair, New Jersey: Boynton/Cook Publishers, 1987.

Atwell, Nancie (Editor). *Coming to Know: Writing to Learn in the Intermediate Grades.* Portsmouth, NH: Heinemann, 1990. Wow! I'm impressed! This book contains a 17 page compilation of successful prompts for learning log entries.

A Learner's Journal

Topic _____

Name _____

Date _____

Teacher Comments	
	_____
	_____
	_____
	_____
	_____
	_____
	_____
	_____
	_____
	_____
	_____
	_____
	_____
	_____
	_____
	_____
	_____
	_____
	_____
	_____
	_____
	_____

Journal Jottings

Virginia DeBolt: *Write! Cooperative Learning and the Writing Process*
Kagan Cooperative Learning • 1 (800) WEE CO-OP

MR. Happy Face
123 Joy Ln.
U.S.A.

The Great Send-Off

Lesson-at-a-Glance

Grades	Academic Skills	Time
3 - 6	• Correct use of parts of letter • Addressing envelopes correctly • Locating selected resources • Writing letters requesting materials	1-3 weeks

Materials

- Names & addresses of tourist attractions & organizations
- Envelopes & stamps
- Formation Cards Handout
- One Letter Parts & Envelope Parts reproducible per team
- Two 9 x 12 sheets construction paper per team

Strand
Functional

Structures
- **Chalkboard Share**
- **Formations**
- **Independent Writing**
- **Pairs Confer**
- **Team Discussion**
- **Think-Write-Pair-Compare**

Lesson Overview

In this lesson, the student will review correct letter and envelope format. The student will write and mail a letter to an organization or agency related to your curriculum. The letter will request information and materials for students to use in your classroom.

Designate the first week or two of the school year "The Great Send-Off." During this time have students write requesting information from any organization relevant to the curriculum for your grade. Many sources provide free posters, maps, brochures, and speakers. The

Great Send-Off gives students a reason to write real letters, and it adds the excitement of awaiting and receiving the mail. We teachers are such pack rats, aren't we? You probably have a perfectly wonderful poster of the bats in Carlsbad Caverns already, don't you? Well, resist the temptation to dig it out and hand it to a kid. Make her write to ask for a copy.

Children enjoy practicing correct envelope formats if you set up a mail box in your classroom. Provide a supply of letter and legal sized envelopes. Give every student in the room an address, for example: Jane Doe, The Junky Jokers, #3, Room 8, Hillcrest School. Deliver only properly addressed mail and mark improperly addressed envelopes "Return to Sender."

Virginia DeBolt: *Write! Cooperative Learning and the Writing Process*
Kagan Cooperative Learning • 1 (800) WEE CO-OP

99

Lesson Sequence

Prewrite

Format a letter using
Team Discussion

Each team should appoint the following: materials monitor, cutter, paster, researcher. The materials monitor will distribute two sheets of construction paper (a different color for each team) and one copy of the reproducible letter and envelope parts, page 105-107, to each team. As the cutter cuts the letter and envelope forms into separate parts, the researcher looks in an English book or English Handbook for the placement of letter parts on the page. One sheet of construction paper represents a large letter, the other a large envelope. The team places the individual letter and envelope parts in appropriate positions on the construction papers. Before the paster can glue the pieces down, the entire team must agree that the placement is correct.

Share letter format using
Chalkboard Share

At the teacher's signal, the materials monitor brings the completed construction paper forms to the board and tapes or tacks them up for display.

Give teams time to study and comment on the forms.

Plan a letter using
Think-Write-Pair-Compare

Assign each student one or more addresses to use in writing individual letters.

The teacher asks, "Think: What do the people to whom we write have to know in order to understand what we want and to be willing to send it to us?" Have each student write the information they deem important for the body of the letter. Pair: share the list with a partner. Compare: the pair may take some time to share with other pairs. Each student saves the list to use when writing.

Write

Write a letter using
Independent Writing

Students prepare the first drafts.

Confer

Confer on content using
Pairs Confer

Pairs confer about questions such as: Will the reader understand what I'm requesting? Is my letter clear? Is my request polite? Have I included all the important information? Students make needed revisions.

Proof/Edit

Editing Conference using
Pairs Confer

Students pair up for another conference concerned with letter form, spelling, and other mechanics. They prepare a clean copy of their letter and submit it for a teacher editing conference. Although a teacher edit is not always desirable, it's never too soon to teach the children that writing we send out into the world for public reading should be technically correct. Invented spelling is OK in the classroom process, but in a letter to the governor, it's a no-no. Following the teacher conference, students make a final draft.

Publish

Mail the letter.

Useful Addresses

The **World Almanac** is readily available in elementary schools. It contains addresses

Virginia DeBolt: *Write! Cooperative Learning and the Writing Process*
Kagan Cooperative Learning • 1 (800) WEE CO-OP

of state Chambers of Commerce, corporations, and foreign embassies.

National Societies

National Audubon Society
 613 Riversville Road
 Greenwich, CT 06831
National Dairy Council
 Rosemont, Il 60018
National Geographic Society
 Educational Services, Dept. 5250
 Washington, D.C. 20036
National Wildlife Federation
 1412 Sixteenth Street N.W.
 Washington, D.C. 20036
Museum of Fine Arts
 465 Huntington Ave.
 Boston, Mass. 02115
Reading & O'reilly
 Box 302
 Wilton, CT, 06897
 (art and art history, filmstrips)

Local Resources

Aquariums, Architects, Artists, Camps, Museums, Colleges and Universities, Department of Public Works, 4-H Clubs, Garden Clubs, Historical Societies, Humane Societies, Libraries, Lumber Yards, Newspapers, Nurseries and Florists, Planetariums, Realtors, Safety and Law Enforcement Agencies, State Government, Travel Agencies, Utilities, Veterinarians

National Parks

The following list of National Parks does not include street addresses. However, letters addressed to Park Headquarters at these locations would probably arrive.

Acadia National Park
 Bar Harbor, Maine 04609
Arches National Park
 Moab, Utah 84532
Badlands National Park
 Wall, South Dakota 57790

Big Bend National Park
 Persimmon Gap, Texas
Biscayne National Park
 Key Biscayne, Florida 33149
Bryce Canyon National Park
 Bryce Canyon, Utah 84717
Canyonlands National Park
 Moab, Utah 84532
Capitol Reef National Park
 Torrey, Utah 84775
Carlsbad Caverns National Park
 Carlsbad, New Mexico 88220
Channel Islands National Park
 Santa Barbara, California 93100
Crater Lake National Park
 Medford, Oregon 97503
Denali National Park
 Anderson, Alaska 99744
Everglades National Park
 Homestead, Florida 33034
Gates of the Arctic National Park
 Wiseman, Alaska
Glacier Bay National Park
 Yakutat, Alaska 99689
Glacier National Park
 West Glacier, Montana 59936
Grand Canyon National Park
 Grand Canyon, Arizona 86023
Grand Teton National Park
 Moose, Wyoming 83012
Great Smoky Mountains National Park
 Gatlinburg, Tennessee 37738
Guadalupe Mountains National Park
 Pine Springs, Texas
Heleakala National Park
 Kahului, Maui, Hawaii 96732
Hawaii Volcanoes National Park
 Island of Hawaii 96718
Hot Springs National Park
 Hot Springs, Arkansas 71909
Isle Royal National Park
 Houghton, Michigan 49931
Katmai National Park
 King Salmon, Alaska 99613

Kenai Fjords National Park
Kenai, Alaska 99611
Kings Canyon National Park
Fresno, California 93700
Kobuk Valley National Park
Kotzebue, Alaska 99752
Lake Clark National Park
Anchorage, Alaska 99500
Lassen Volcanic National Park
Susanville, California 96130
Mammoth Cave National Park
Mammoth Cave, Kentucky 42259
Mesa Verde National Park
Mesa Verde, Colorado 81330
Mount Rainier National Park
Longmire, Washington 98397
North Cascades National Park
Marblemount, Washington 98267
Olympic National Park
Port Angeles, Washington 98362
Petrified Forest National Park
Holbrook, Arizona 86028
Platt National Park
Sulphur, Oklahoma 73086
Redwood National Park
Orick, California 95555
Rocky Mountain National Park
Estes Park, Colorado 80517
Sequoia National Park
Three Rivers, California 93271
Shenandoah National Park
Luray, Virginia 22835
Theodore Roosevelt Memorial
National Park
Medora, North Dakota 58645
Virgin Islands National Park
St. John, U.S. Virgin Islands 00800
Voyageurs National Park
Kabetogama Minnesota
Wind Cave National Park
Hot Springs, South Dakota 57747
Wrangell-St. Elias National Park
Cordova, Alaska 99574

Yellowstone National Park
Yellowstone, Wyoming 82190
Yosemite National Park
Yosemite Village, California 95389
Zion National Park
Springdale, Utah 84763

Alternative Activities

Prewrite

Form a living letter using *Formations*

Reproduce the Formation cards on pages 108-114. Thirteen cards are needed for a friendly letter, eighteen for a business letter. Give a student a card and he or she then becomes that part of the letter. Students without cards should link-up. (Grade level and teacher judgment will determine how they link up. Kids could hook arms, hold hands, put hands on hips or shoulders in a "conga line", touch fingertips, or go elbow to elbow.) The linked-up bunch join the person with the Body formation card. A large body of bodies will create a Body.

Take the class to an open space in the gym or outside. Children with a formation card bring it. Specify what part of the space represents the top of the paper. Ask students to form themselves into a letter without speaking. When every student is in place, cardholders call out what they are. If any students with parts of the letter are lost or misplaced, the class could help them find their way to the correct spot with a game like "Hot or Cold." ("You're getting warm. Warmer. You're hot. You're a red hot comma!")

Virginia DeBolt: *Write! Cooperative Learning and the Writing Process*

102　　Kagan Cooperative Learning • 1 (800) WEE CO-OP

Grades 1-6

The Great Send-Off

Letter Parts

Directions: Cut on the lines. Shuffle the pieces, and then correctly place the parts of a letter on another paper.

Heading

Street

City, State, Zip Code

Date

Greeting

Dear _____,

Body

Write message here. Write message here.
Write message here. Write message here.

Write message here. Write message here.
Write message here. Write message here.

Closing
and
Signature

Yours truly,

_____

Grades 4-6

The Great Send-Off

Business Letter Parts

Directions: Cut out the letter parts. Arrange them in the correct positions on another paper.

Date

Date

Street

City, State, Zip Code

Date

Heading

Name

Street

Inside
Address

City, State, Zip Code

Dear _____,

Greeting

Write message here. Write message here.
Write message here. Write message here.

Write message here. Write message here.
Write message here. Write message here.

Body

Yours truly,

Closing
and
Signature

_____

Virginia DeBolt: *Write! Cooperative Learning and the Writing Process*
Kagan Cooperative Learning • 1 (800) WEE CO-OP

104

Grades 1-6

The Great Send-Off

Envelope Parts

Directions: Cut out the two parts of an envelope. Place them in the correct locations on an envelope or another paper.

Return
Address

> **Sender's Name**
>
> **Sender's Street**
>
> **Sender's City, State, Zip Code**

Address

> **Name**
>
> **Street**
>
> **City, State, Zip Code**

Virginia DeBolt: *Write! Cooperative Learning and the Writing Process*
Kagan Cooperative Learning • 1 (800) WEE CO-OP

105

Formation Cards

**Street number
and name
or
Post office box
number**

City

Virginia DeBolt: *Write! Cooperative Learning and the Writing Process*
Kagan Cooperative Learning • 1 (800) WEE CO-OP

State & Zip Code

Month & Day

Virginia DeBolt: *Write! Cooperative Learning and the Writing Process*

Kagan Cooperative Learning • 1 (800) WEE CO-OP

107

Formation Cards

Dear _____

Body

Your friend

Virginia DeBolt: *Write! Cooperative Learning and the Writing Process*

Kagan Cooperative Learning • 1 (800) WEE CO-OP

109

Formation Cards

Signature

(Business Letter)

Name

(Business Letter)

Street number and name

Virginia DeBolt: *Write! Cooperative Learning and the Writing Process*

Kagan Cooperative Learning • 1 (800) WEE CO-OP

110

(Business Letter)

City

(Business Letter)

(Business Letter)

State & Zip Code

Virginia DeBolt: *Write! Cooperative Learning and the Writing Process*
Kagan Cooperative Learning • 1 (800) WEE CO-OP

111

Formation Cards

(Business Letter)

Greeting

(Business Letter)

●

●

(Business Letter)

Closing

Letters & Envelopes

Peer Response

MR. Hoppy Face
123 Joy Ln.
U.S.A.

Gambits:

1. I understand what you are requesting: it is _____ _____

2. The person receiving the letter might want to know _____ _____ _____ .

First Things First

Lesson-at-a-Glance

Grades	Academic Skills	Time
3 - 6	Writing paragraphs showing time order	1 or 2 class periods

Materials	Strand
• Basic writing materials	Functional

Lesson Overview

In this lesson, the student will role play, make notes and write a paragraph describing an activity that must be done in a particular order. The student will learn to use time order words such as first, next, and last.

Young writers tend to show time order with, "and then, so, but, and, and, and." Make students sensitive to these words by forbidding them for a day as sentence openers.

Time order words are valuable as transitions. Used well, they save readers from the boring details. For example, a simple, "After breakfast, I..." spares readers from the mundane details of waking, rising, dressing, and eating that children might otherwise use to begin a story.

Lesson Sequence

Prewrite

Find topics using *Inside-Outside Circle*

Students stand in an Inside-Outside Circle, each facing a partner. Every student has a pad on which to record ideas. Each child in the pair names one activity he or she does in a particular order. Students record these ideas. Both circles rotate one person to the right and repeat the process with a new pair and a new idea. After five or more rotations, students have produced and collected many topic ideas about ordered activities. Students return to home teams.

List activities in order using *Write-What-I-Act*

Tell students, "Pair up to role play a three or four step activity. An example might be putting on socks, then shoes, then tying the shoes." Students write up what they watch

- • *Class Brainstorming*
- • *Independent Writing*
- • *Inside-Outside Circle*
- • *Roam the Room*
- • *Roundrobin*
- • *Roundtable*
- • *Write-What-I-Act*

Structures

Virginia DeBolt: *Write! Cooperative Learning and the Writing Process*
Kagan Cooperative Learning • 1 (800) WEE CO-OP

115

their partner act out, practicing time order words as they write.

Write

Write time order paragraphs using *Independent Writing*

Each student writes a time order paragraph using the notes his partner made during Write-What-I-Act.

Confer

Confer on content using *Roundrobin*

Prepare for the Roundrobin by discussing again the goal of effective presentation of an idea in time order. Spend two or three minutes eliciting gambit suggestions from students that might be used during the Roundrobin conference. Then each student reads his or her writing to teammates who respond with praisers, questions or suggestions.

Proof/Edit

Editing Conference using *Roundtable*

Within teams, the students pass the written work around from teammate to teammate to be edited for spelling, punctuation, capitalization and other mechanics. Following the Roundtable, each writer prepares a final draft.

Publish

Celebrate authors using *Roam the Room*

Final drafts are displayed on desktops. A feedback sheet for recording the signed praisers is placed next to the writing. Students roam the room reading others' work

and recording praisers. The teacher decides whether to place a limit on the number of desks each child will visit. When this activity is complete, place all drafts of the work in the assessment portfolios.

Alternative Activities

Prewrite

Time Line using *Independent Writing*

Use a simple time line to organize the ideas generated in the Inside-Outside Circle. See sample Time Line.

Generate time order words using *Class Brainstorming*

Take two or three minutes to list time order words on the chalkboard. Students might suggest words such as: first, second, then, next, last, finally, before, after, soon, while.

9:00 PM	go to sleep
8:30	bath time / TV time
6:30	dinner time / do homework / play / change clothes / tease my sister
3:00	eat something
2:50	go home
12:00	FOOD!!
10:30	RECESS!!
8:25	tardy bell / tease my sister
8:06	go to school
8:05	grab homework / brush teeth / tease my sister
7:30	eat breakfast / dress
7:00 AM	wake up

Sample Time Line

Virginia DeBolt: *Write! Cooperative Learning and the Writing Process*

116   Kagan Cooperative Learning • 1 (800) WEE CO-OP

Time Line

pm

am

Virginia DeBolt: *Write! Cooperative Learning and the Writing Process*
Kagan Cooperative Learning • 1 (800) WEE CO-OP

117

Time Order Paragraphs

Peer Response

Title _____

Name _____

_____

_____

_____

_____

_____

_____

_____

_____

_____

_____

_____

_____

_____

_____

_____

_____

_____

_____

_____

_____

_____

_____

_____

Gambits:

1. I knew your events were in order because _____
_____.

2. You need another step where _____
_____
_____.

Virginia DeBolt: *Write! Cooperative Learning and the Writing Process*

118 Kagan Cooperative Learning • 1 (800) WEE CO-OP

Descriptive Paragraphs

Chapter 13

The Way I See It

Lesson-at-a-Glance

Grades	Academic Skills	Time
3 - 6	Writing paragraphs that describe a scene from near to far or from far to near	2 - 3 periods

Materials
- Basic writing materials
- 1 large piece construction paper per team
- 1 poster board per team
- Camera and film

Strand
Functional

Structures
- **Team Brainstorm**
- **Draw-What-I-Write**
- **Independent Writing**
- **Inside-Outside Circle**
- **Simultaneous Roundtable**
- **Team Posters**

Lesson Overview

Tell students they will be going on a walk or trip to view a setting outside the classroom. While there, they will make notes or a list recording what they see, hear, and smell. The descriptive spiders worksheet, page 126, might be useful in recording sensory impressions. A list should be written from near to far, or from far to near. While at the site, the teacher photographs the scene the students will be describing. Take enough pictures, or make enough prints, so that every team will have a photo.

Lesson Sequence

Prewrite
Generate space order words using **Team Brainstorm**

On construction paper, each team brainstorms a list of phrases that will aid in describing space order. Phrases might include: nearby, in front of, in the distance, overhead, underfoot, on the horizon. Post the phrases in the room for everyone to see.

Write
Write space order paragraphs using **Independent Writing**

Students work independently to write paragraphs describing the site or picture selected. The description moves through space in an ordered fashion, either from near to far, or from far to near.

Confer
Confer on content using **Inside-Outside Circle**

Students stand facing a partner in an Inside-Outside Circle. The pair read their paragraphs to each other, then offer helpful comments or questions. Students take notes so they can later improve their paragraph. Both circles do a right-face and walk forward two people. The students pair up again with a new partner and repeat the revising conference. Thus, each child receives feedback from two others about his paragraph. Back at their desks, students make changes and revisions.

Proof/Edit

Editing Conference using
Simultaneous Roundtable

Within teams, students pass their work to their teammates for proofreading and editing. Each piece receives attention from three helpers before it returns to its owner.

Publish

Celebrate Authors using
Team Posters

Provide each team with a sheet of poster board and photos from the scene. Teams prepare a display of their writing and the photos. Display the finished posters in the room or halls.

Lesson Extension

Setting is an important aspect of story telling. Be sure to connect the skill of describing an environment with writing stories.

Alternative Activities

Prewrite

Generate detail words using
Team Discussion

Provide each team with a least one picture you took at the site. Say, "List every detail about the place you are describing. Use the

picture to help you remember how it looked. Use your notes from the trip."

If it was impossible for you to take your class on an excursion for this lesson, an interesting and detailed picture or poster can be substituted. Use the same techniques to collect space order words and descriptive details.

Eat What You Write

Bring in enough oranges, or bananas, or unshelled peanuts for the entire class. Give one to each student. The student must write a description of his or her own apple or peanut. Use Mix-Freeze-Group to move all the students, who are toting with them their description and their food item, to new groups. Groups of six work well. All the oranges are piled in the center of the group. Descriptions are exchanged Roundtable fashion. Each student's task is to find the particular orange described on the paper he or she is reading. When the foods are correctly coupled with the descriptions, everyone retrieves his or her original item and description, returns to home base, and eats the evidence.

Practice using space order using *Draw-What-I-Write*

Draw simple pictures, such as the two illustrated on the following page, on the board. Tell students, "Draw a simple picture such as these showing objects arranged from near to far. Working alone, so that no one can see your drawing, write a space order

> *"As my gaze moved to the tree by my side I found myself looking into the bulging black eyes of a huge spider."*

Virginia DeBolt: *Write! Cooperative Learning and the Writing Process*

120   Kagan Cooperative Learning • 1 (800) WEE CO-OP

paragraph describing what you drew."
When the paragraphs are finished, have the
students return to teams and work in pairs.
Say, "Now, without showing your partner
your picture, read your paragraph to your
partner so that he or she can attempt to
reproduce what you drew."

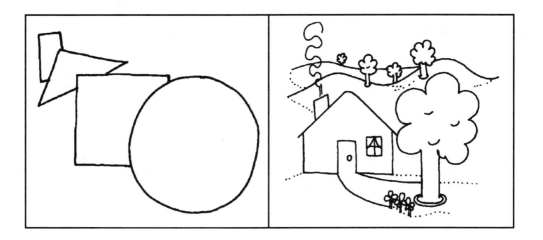

Virginia DeBolt: *Write! Cooperative Learning and the Writing Process*

Kagan Cooperative Learning • 1 (800) WEE CO-OP   **121**

Descriptive Spiders

Name _____

Directions: Add words at the ends of the spiders' legs to help you describe a scene.

SEE

FEEL

HEAR

SMELL

TASTE

Virginia DeBolt: *Write! Cooperative Learning and the Writing Process*

122   Kagan Cooperative Learning • 1 (800) WEE CO-OP

Samplings

The Lady in the Mist

On one Hollaween night there were kids trick-or-treating. They arrived at this one old house where nobody lived. The old house had rotten flowers and a horrible looking gate, it looked like the gate had been chewed up by termites. The old house looked one hundred years old. The old house had mist surrounding the creepy area.

"Who wants to go knock first." Jason said.

"Whhat's thhhat!" Patrick stammered.

"It looks like a women in the mist!" Jason said ecited.

"It looks like she went in the door. Steven said.

"Don't you mean went through the door' Arnold said in a scared trilling voice...

Adrian Garcia
Gr. 5 Hillcrest School
Carlsbad, NM

Virginia DeBolt: *Write! Cooperative Learning and the Writing Process*

Kagan Cooperative Learning • 1 (800) WEE CO-OP

123

Descriptive Paragraphs

Peer Response	Title _____
	Name _____

_____

_____

_____

_____

_____

_____

_____

_____

_____

_____

_____

_____

_____

_____

_____

_____

_____

_____

_____

_____

_____

_____

_____

_____

Gambits:

1. I really imagined what it looked like when I read

_____

_____.

2. You really involved all my senses by _____

_____

_____.

Virginia DeBolt: *Write! Cooperative Learning and the Writing Process*

124   Kagan Cooperative Learning • 1 (800) WEE CO-OP

Compare and Contrast

Bicycles &
Boomerangs

Lesson-at-a-Glance

Grades	Academic Skills	Time
3 - 6	• Indenting Paragraphs • Developing a Main Idea Sentence • Using Supporting Details • Taking Notes	2 - 3 lessons

Materials

• 1 large piece white construction paper per team
• Carbon Paper

Strand

Functional

Lesson Overview

This lesson treats the concepts of comparison and contrast as two separate ideas. Each is written about in its own paragraph, with a main idea sentence. Circles and rectangles are used to distinguish likeness and difference in a word web, to help children separate the two concepts into paragraphs.

Lesson Sequence

Prewrite

Generate comparisons using *Roundtable Word Web*

Using one sheet of construction paper per team, have the students create a word web comparing and contrasting eagles and canaries. Students pass the paper around the table to each team member in turn until the team has generated at least three ways in which eagles and canaries are alike, and three ways in which they are different. Let them represent "alike" and "different" using circles to show similarities and squares to show differences. A team might create a web such as the one on the following page.

Write

Write collaboratively using *Team Discussion*

Teammates agree on a main idea sentence for a paragraph comparing eagles with canaries. Have the team recorder frame three circled ideas from the word web as three detail sentences showing similarities between eagles and canaries.

To complete the second paragraph, repeat the process of writing a main idea sentence and three detail sentences contrasting the two birds.

- *Roundtable Word Web*
- *Team Discussion*
- *Teams Consult*
- *Carbon Sharing*
- *Rotating Feedback*
- *Partners*

Structures

Virginia DeBolt: *Write! Cooperative Learning and the Writing Process*

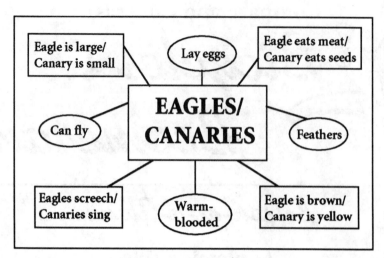

Eagle is large/ Canary is small

Lay eggs

Eagle eats meat/ Canary eats seeds

Can fly

EAGLES/ CANARIES

Feathers

Eagles screech/ Canaries sing

Warm-blooded

Eagle is brown/ Canary is yellow

Confer

Confer on content using *Teams Consult*

Teams share their paragraphs with the team next to them, using a Team Reader. Teams then assist each other with suggestions regarding clarity, the use of complete sentences, or other areas needing improvement.

Allow time for revision and for teams to produce a clean copy and a carbon copy.

Proof/Edit

Proofreading exchange using *Carbon Sharing*

The carbon copy is given to another team. Each team works to detect errors in spelling or mechanics. Resource materials (the dictionary, the English Handbook) may be used freely. Proofreading and editing suggestions are marked on the carbon copy, which is then returned to the original team.

Allow time for each team to make corrections and to rewrite as necessary.

Publish

Display paragraphs using *Rotating Feedback*

Post the finished paragraphs on the chalkboard or the bulletin board. A feedback sheet is posted under each composition. Allow teams to tour the room, reading the paragraphs of other teams. Praise, comments, congratulations, and suggestions are written on the feedback sheets.

Lesson Extension

Individual Assessment

Assign individuals another two-paragraph compare and contrast composition on ideas such as: jet fighters/bullfrogs; Eddie Murphy/Donald Duck; Judy Blume/Stephen King; my allowance/Disneyland; a book/a hot fudge sundae. Have each individual turn in evidence of prewriting, rewriting or revising, and editing. The paragraphs are published by turning them in to the teacher.

Virginia DeBolt: *Write! Cooperative Learning and the Writing Process*

126   Kagan Cooperative Learning • 1 (800) WE CO-OP

Collaborate on a report using *Partners*

Use Partners to compare and contrast. The material provided here for Partners gives the students additional experience writing in collaboration with another student. The Partners design is extremely powerful for two reasons. It motivates learning more effectively than any teaching method I have experienced. It creates a sense of positive interdependence among teammates because each student has a unique contribution to make to the learning goal.

Powerful Motivator
Positive Interdependence

Partners

The steps of partners can be found in Chapter 5. Partners can be used with any content. Located in this chapter is information needed to use Partners to create a brief collaborative research report about chipmunks and squirrels with the compare and contrast process described in the lesson.

Form partners within teams. Topic 1 partners sit on one side of the room; Topic 2 partners on the other. Distribute copies of the reference materials on squirrels to the Topic 1 partner, chipmunks to the other.

Students work to master their material, consulting with same-topic partners. They plan a teaching strategy for sharing their information with their team partner. They may take notes, prepare visuals, draw diagrams, or use any method they prefer to teach their subject.

Partners reunite and share their information. Have them create a partner word web based on what they have learned from each other about squirrels and chipmunks. Using the word web, partner groups write paragraphs comparing and contrasting the two animals.

Partner groups confer, revise, and edit with the assistance of their teammates. Prewriting, first drafts, and final drafts should all be handed in or displayed in another Gallery Tour.

References

Kagan, Spencer. *Cooperative Learning.* San Juan Capistrano, CA: Kagan Cooperative Learning, 1993.

Reproducible:
Collaborate on a Report using _Partners_

Topic One Partner

Chipmunks

Chipmunks are rodents. They have the big front teeth to prove it. Those useful teeth help them crack open nuts and seeds. Chipmunks also like to eat berries, beetles, frogs, and eggs.

Chipmunks gather and store food in underground pantries. They may have half a bushel of nuts and other food stored in their burrow. That's about the same as half a laundry basket of food. It's plenty of food to get the tiny chipmunk through the winter. Chipmunks sleep for about 3 months during the winter. They sometimes wake up and move around a little on warm winter days.

Chipmunks weigh about 4 1/2 ounces. They are about 8 inches long, including the tail. They have reddish-brown fur. There are four light colored stripes bordered in black running down their backs. There are 17 species of chipmunks. Chipmunks are members of the same family as squirrels. Female chipmunks have from 2 to 8 young twice a year. Chipmunks live 2 or 3 years.

Home to a chipmunk is a burrow under a tree or rock. The burrow is 2 or 3 feet deep and might be several yards long. It has several rooms--a pantry, even a "washroom."

Chipmunks live throughout North America from Canada to northern Mexico. They make a scolding sound when people approach, but they are easy to tame. They will take food from a person's hand. They carry food away by stuffing it into their cheeks.

Virginia DeBolt: *Write! Cooperative Learning and the Writing Process*

128   Kagan Cooperative Learning • 1 (800) WE CO-OP

Topic Two Partner

Squirrels

There are 55 species of squirrels. The best known are red squirrels and gray squirrels. They are members of the rodent family. Rodents are gnawing animals with chisel-like front teeth.

Squirrels live in trees. They have large, furry tails which help them balance when leaping from branch to branch. They build homes in hollow tree trunks or the crotch of a tree. If food is scarce, or if there are too many squirrels in one area, they sometimes migrate.

Squirrels eat berries, fruits, nuts, mushrooms and seeds. They store food in holes in trees or in the ground. Sometimes they don't eat the nuts they have hidden in the ground. Those nuts grow into trees. Squirrels help replant the forest by forgetting to go back for hidden food . Red squirrels love to eat pine cones. They might store 3 to 10 bushels of pine cones for the winter.

The red squirrel lives to be 8 or 9 years old. It is about 12 inches long and weighs 1/2 a pound. A gray squirrel may live to be 15. Gray squirrels are about 18 inches long and weigh 1 1/2 pounds. Both kinds give birth twice a year, having 2 to 6 young at a time.

Squirrels chatter and scold when people are near. They can be tamed to take nuts from a person's hand. A person feeding a squirrel needs to be careful not to get bitten. Squirrels can carry diseases that hurt people.

Samplings

Mickey Mouse is like James Dean in many ways. They are both my favorites. They are both popular. They are both actually old, but in the pictures and posters of them, they look young. Both of them are movie stars. Both of them have many fans.

Mickey Mouse and James Dean are different because Mickey does not have a middle name and James Dean does. Mickey Mouse is a cartoon character and James Dean is an actual human being. Mickey's been in more movies than James Dean. Mickey's still alive. Mickey has a tail and James just has a nice rear. Mickey has a well known partner, Minnie, but James didn't. James smoked and Mickey doesn't. Mickey is well liked by children and James is well liked by adults.

They are different in more ways than they are alike, but that's what makes me like them most.

Betsy Pike
Gr. 8
Carlsbad, NM

Compare & Contrast

Peer Response	Title
	Name

Gambits:

1. I thought it was interesting when you wrote _____ _____ _____.

2. Are there any more ways your subjects are alike? _____ _____ _____

How To's

Lesson-at-a-Glance

Grades	Academic Skills	Time
3 - 6	Giving directions in ordered steps	2 - 3 periods

Materials	Strand
• Basic Writing Materials • Flow Chart Reproducible	Functional

Lesson Overview

In this lesson, the student will act out the steps in an activity, while a partner helps record the steps in order on a flow chart. Using the flow chart, the student will write instructions or directions.

Lesson Sequence

Prewrite
Generate "How To's" using
Roundtable
Students brainstorm using Roundtable to generate as many possible "How To" writing topics as they can, such as, How to Care for Teenagers, Directions for Living Life, How to Hook up a Stereo, How to Eat an Oreo Cookie, etc.

Pantomime directions using
Write-What-I-Act
Have the students work in pairs. As one student silently acts out the steps of his or her instructions, the other student orally interprets what is seen. Then the two work together to complete the simple flow chart, located on the following page, identifying the steps. The second student then acts out his or her directions, and the pair complete a second flow chart.

Write
Write instructions using
Independent Writing
Each student writes directions using the completed flow chart.

Confer
Confer on content using
Pairs Confer
Students pair up with a new partner — one who did not see the Formation or help

- *Think-Write-Pair-Share*
- *Write-What-I-Act*
- *Roundtable*
- *Independent Writing*
- *Pairs Confer*
- *Experts Edit*
- *Roam the Room*

Structures

Virginia DeBolt: *Write! Cooperative Learning and the Writing Process*
Kagan Cooperative Learning • 1 (800) WEE CO-OP

133

prepare the flow chart. The two confer about how well the directions accomplish the task of telling how to do something. Then students return to their desks to work on any necessary revisions.

Proof/Edit

Editing Conference using *Experts Edit*

Select eight students as expert editors. Arrange a work space for them in the four corners of the room. As students complete their revisions, they confer with one of the experts about proofreading and editing.

Publish

Celebrate authors using *Roam the Room*

Students prepare a final copy. Have them save the flow chart and first draft with revisions in individual writing folders. Display the final copies in the room. Give students a few days to read others' directions, then add the final copies to the folders.

Alternative Activities

Prewrite

Kagan Cooperative Learning publishes *Same-Different: Holidays Edition* by Spencer Kagan and *Match Mine* by Laurie Robertson. Using activities from either of these resources before writing instructions on paper will be fun and produce a great deal of language development. Students learn that precise language is necessary for successful directions.

Learner's Journal instructions using *Think-Write-Pair-Share*

Use the student's journal to provide frequent practice in writing instructions and directions. Tell them, "Explain how you comb your hair. Then pair up with a buddy and read each other's instructions." Allow students who volunteer to share their writing. Other possible prompts are, "Explain how to exit during a fire drill. Explain how to complement a teammate. Give directions for walking to the office from our room. How would you instruct a 2nd grader if you had to teach him or her to borrow in subtraction?"

Generate word lists using *Roundtable*

Have each team brainstorm a list of as many direction ordering words as possible. The list might include: first, second, third, next, finally, then ...

References

Kagan, Spencer. *Same-Different: Holidays Edition.* San Juan Capistrano, CA: Kagan Cooperative Learning, 1992.

Robertson, Laurie. *Match Mine.* San Juan Capistrano, CA: Kagan Cooperative Learning, 1991.

Virginia DeBolt: *Write! Cooperative Learning and the Writing Process*
Kagan Cooperative Learning • 1 (800) WEE CO-OP

134

Writing Instructions and Directions

Name _____

Directions: List the steps of your instructions in order. Use as many boxes as you need. Add more boxes if you need them.

Topic

Step 1

Step 2

Step 3

Step 4

Step 5

Step 6

Step 7

Samplings

How To Get a Boyfriend

The way you can get a boyfriend is simple. First, you tell the boy that you like him.

Then, show the boy you like him by playing the sport he likes, maybe by agreeing with his comments, or maybe walking beside him and talking to him...

Stacy Snow
Gr. 5 Hillcrest School
Carlsbad, NM

How to Make a Peanut Butter and Jelly Sandwich

Making a peanut butter and jelly sandwich is very easy. First you open the bread and get two pieces out.

Next you get one clean butter knife out of the drawer.

After you get the knife out, open the peanut butter and spread it on one side of one piece of bread.

Then you lick the peanut butter off the knife. When the knife has most of the peanut butter off, you stick it in the jelly jar. Once you've got jelly on your knife, spread it on the other piece of bread. The only thing is, you can't let your mom see you licking the knife.

When you've done all the steps put the two pieces of bread together with the peanut butter and the jelly between the two pieces of bread. After all this you get to eat your sandwich while you're cleaning up your mess.

Lisa Sullivan
Gr. 5 Hillcrest School
Carlsbad, NM

HOW TO INSULT YOUR BIG SISTER

Michael Tackitt

1. Go to the Carlsbad Public Library
2. Get a new book about insults.
3. Go home.
4. Study the book.
5. Rehurse the insults you have learned to yourself.
6. Find your big sister
7. Let her have it!

Michael Tackitt
Gr. 5 Hillcrest School
Carlsbad, NM

Virginia DeBolt: *Write! Cooperative Learning and the Writing Process*

136   Kagan Cooperative Learning • 1 (800) WEE CO-OP

Sampl ngs

The Box Book

Casey Williams
Gr. 6 Alta Vista Middle School
Carlsbad, NM

Cover

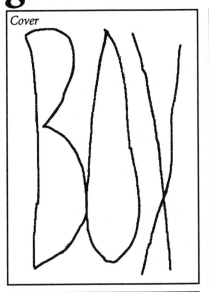

Notes:
fold on the dotted lines.

Start with a square sheet of paper.

fold in half.

fold both ends to the middle.

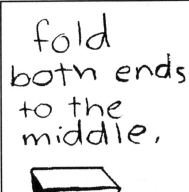

fold corners down

fold ends back so that the ends of the corners

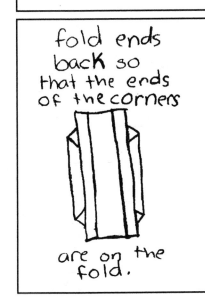

are on the fold.

Pull apart and you have a box.

Back Cover

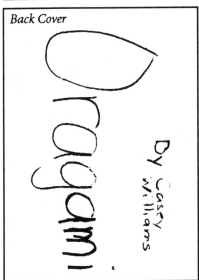

Origami

By Casey Williams

Virginia DeBolt: *Write! Cooperative Learning and the Writing Process*
Kagan Cooperative Learning • 1 (800) WEE CO-OP

137

Instructions & Directions

Title _____

Name _____

Virginia DeBolt: *Write! Cooperative Learning and the Writing Process*

138   Kagan Cooperative Learning • 1 (800) WEE CO-OP

The Literary Guild

Lesson-at-a-Glance

Grades	Academic Skills	Time
3 - 6	Reporting on and evaluating literature	2 - 3 sessions

Materials	Strand
• Basic Writing Materials • Other materials depending on choice of report genre	Nonfiction/Reporting

Lesson Overview

In this lesson, students will create a bank of ideas for interesting new ways to write book reports. Students will use a reproducible to write a book report in the form of a picture post card.

So many clever, interesting, and unusual ideas exist for writing book reports. Book reports can be written as letters to the teacher, as picture post cards, as learning log entries, as book jackets, as plays, as puppet shows, as advertisements, as reviews for school newspapers, as part of a student's research into a favorite author or series, or even the old standard report listing title, author and plot summary.

Have the class generate as many ideas for ways of writing book reports as possible. Write the ideas on the reproducible provided or on pages from oversize spirals or sheets of tagboard. Post the list permanently in a prominent spot in the classroom. When a student writes regularly required written book reports, he or she can refer to the posted list for fresh ideas as to genre. By allowing such choice, the teacher encourages more creativity and complexity in written book reports. You will find helpful reproducibles at the end of the chapter. Use the post card reproducible for this lesson.

Lesson Sequence

Prewrite
Oral book reports using **Team Interview**

Once a week, perhaps the day before library books are due, have the children conduct Team Interviews. Within teams, each child

- **Team Interview**
- **Independent Writing**
- **Pairs Confer**
- **Mix-Freeze-Group**

Structures

stands in turn to talk about the book he or she read during the preceding week. Announce a predetermined time limit for each interview: a minute and a half or two minutes. The student will tell the book's title and author, give a brief synopsis, and a quick evaluation. Teammates may then interview the student regarding points of interest about the book.

As the weeks pass, the students will share books and reading experiences as a result of the weekly conversation about books. You will have created literary circles in the classroom — circles of literate readers who enjoy sharing ideas and opinions about their reading with each other.

Write
Write book report using *Independent Writing*

Each student works independently to write his or her book report, using the post card reproducible.

Confer
Confer on content using *Pairs Confer*

In pairs, students read the reports aloud to help each other with issues such as clarity of meaning, completeness of information, and interest to the reader. Reemphasize that students use positive gambits while critiquing. Provide time for revision.

Proof/Edit
Editing Conference using *Pairs Confer*

In the pairs used during revision, students help each other with the mechanics of proofreading and editing. Each writer then prepares his or her final draft.

Publish
The student turns in the book report to the teacher.

Lesson Extension

Use the Learner's Journal as a way to develop literate readers by having students write comments on any oral or silent reading that occurs in the classroom. Sharing and discussing books informally throughout the day will add to a child's ability to react thoughtfully to any reading/book report assignment.

Alternative Activities

Mix-Freeze-Group is a good structure for oral book reports, if variety is needed.

Teacher Note: **Book Clubs — The Literary Connection**
Are nine of your fourth graders passing Babysitter Club books quickly from hand to hand? Why not put them together in a book discussion group? They can learn the joy of conversation about good stories and practice reporting on books at the same time.

Book Report Marathon

Once a semester let the kids create a major production for the best reading of the semester. This could result in songs, videos, puppet shows, art displays — the sky's the limit.

Ways to Give a Book Report

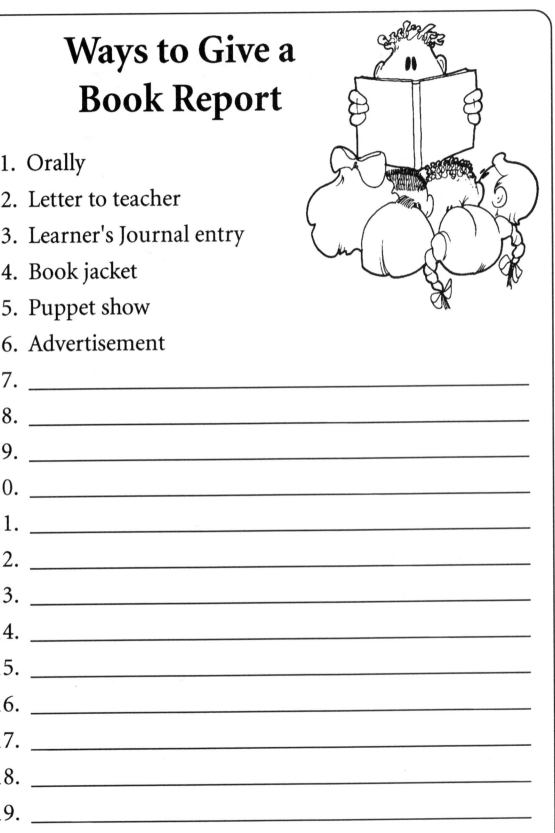

1. Orally
2. Letter to teacher
3. Learner's Journal entry
4. Book jacket
5. Puppet show
6. Advertisement
7. _____
8. _____
9. _____
10. _____
11. _____
12. _____
13. _____
14. _____
15. _____
16. _____
17. _____
18. _____
19. _____
20. _____

BIO-Poem Book Report

Student's Name_____

Date_____

Book_____

Author_____

Character's first name only_____

Four traits that describe character_____

_____

Sibling of (or son of, daughter of)_____

Lover of (three people or ideas)_____

Who feels (three responses)_____

Who needs (three responses)_____

Who gives (three responses)_____

Who fears (three responses)_____

Who would like to see (three responses)_____

Who lives at/in_____

Character's last name only_____

Post Card Book Report

Name_____

Date_____

	Place Postage Here
	_____
	_____
	_____
	_____

Book Title: _____

Author: _____

Dear _____,

_____

_____

_____

_____

Signed, _____

Book Jacket

Name _____

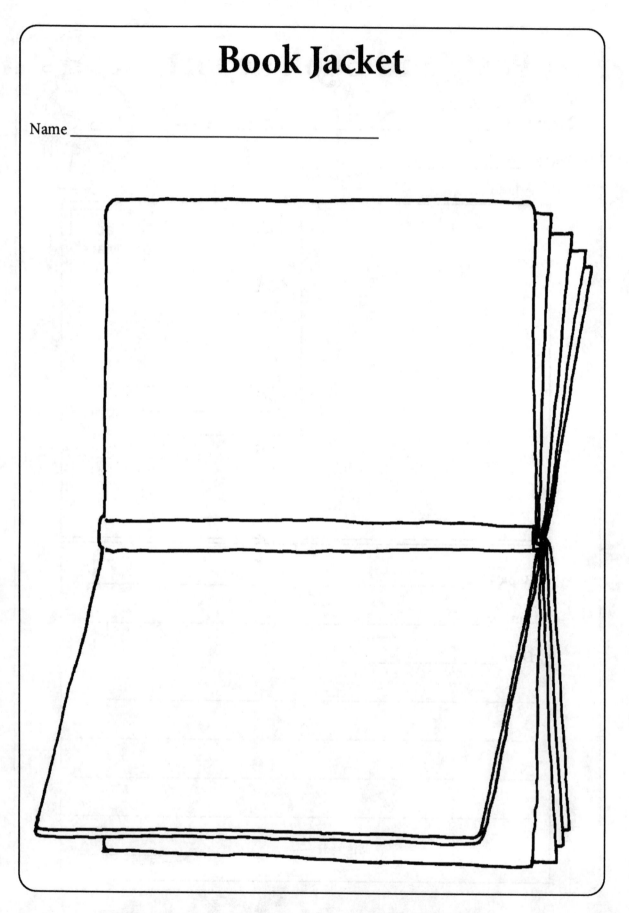

Samplings

The Trip I Took To Bookland

One afternoon I was reading a book and I thought, "You know it would be neat to be at the concert Jessica and Elizabeth went to in the book I was reading called 'Jessica the Rockstar.'

Then I began to think about other books I had read. I thought about so many books that it was like I took a trip.

The first place I went was to Oz. Dorothy asked all her friends to come to a tea party in the beautiful castle so I could meet all of them.

Next I went to Kristy's house. ("The Babysitter's Club," books.) They were in a meeting, so I got to meet all of the members except Stacey. She was sick....

Lisa Sullivan
Gr. 5 Hillcrest School
Carlsbad, NM

Virginia DeBolt: *Write! Cooperative Learning and the Writing Process*
Kagan Cooperative Learning • 1 (800) WEE CO-OP

145

Book Report

Peer Response

Title _____

Name _____

_____

_____

_____

_____

_____

_____

_____

_____

_____

_____

_____

_____

_____

_____

_____

_____

_____

_____

_____

_____

_____

Gambits:

1. Do you know any more about your book (or author)?

_____

2. The part where you said

_____

_____

made me want to read the book.

Virginia DeBolt: *Write! Cooperative Learning and the Writing Process*

Kagan Cooperative Learning • 1 (800) WEE CO-OP

146

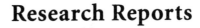

Research Reports

I Search

Lesson-at-a-Glance

Grades	Academic Skills	Time
3 - 6	Researching, applying, organizing and presenting information	4 - 6 weeks

Materials
- Books
- Films
- Filmstrips
- Maps
- List of people, museums, parks, libraries, government bodies

Strand
Nonfiction/Reporting

Lesson Overview

In this lesson, students will work in teams on mini-topics related to an overall theme or topic. The project will take many weeks or more to complete. Students, with the support of teammates, will work individually to research their particular mini-topic. Students will record the results of their learning in daily journaling periods. Then, together with teammates, students will synthesize information and prepare a team presentation for the class.

For this project, pick an aspect of the curriculum that requires several weeks of intensive study. It might be a unit in health, science, social studies, or music. In the lesson design here, the example used is a study of the students' home state.

I Search vs. Research

Kids are capable of original research. It is far more beneficial than copying from the encyclopedia. I personally like the notion of kids writing original field guides for birds, reptiles, insects, and mammals in their local environment. Imagine the enthusiastic response you'd get if you gave 9-year old boys a legitimate excuse to catch blue-tailed lizards for a field guide project.

Co-op Co-op requires that students cooperate within teams to master a topic. Each team then cooperates with the whole class to present its information and contribute to the learning goal of the whole group.

Facilitating Co-op Co-op

Before listing the ten steps of the Co-op Co-op lesson design that the students will do, let's examine the teacher's role. First, prepare a handout indicating the requirements for the project: What is required of each person, of each team? What will be expected in the individual write-ups: tables of contents, bibliographies, notes, final drafts?

Second, plan a daily and weekly schedule. Plan to insert lessons on note taking, interviewing techniques, outlines, library use, bibliographies, and the table of contents at intervals through the duration of the project. A suggested daily schedule might include a five minute status-of-the-class check, an occasional mini-lesson by the teacher, 20 or 30 minutes of individual and group research, and 10 or 15 minutes of writing notes about the day's learning. Plans might include field trips, museum visits, and guest speakers.

The Ten Steps of Co-op Co-op

1. Student-Centered Class Discussion

Students are encouraged to express their knowledge and interests about their own state. The purpose of the discussion is to stimulate interest and curiosity about the subject. Students should begin to identify areas of interest: things they would like to learn or experience about the topic. According to Kagan (1992), "The importance of the initial student-centered discussion cannot be underestimated; it is unlikely that Co-op Co-op will be successful for any students who are not actively interested in a topic related to the unit, and who are not motivated to learn more about the topic."

Students should also realize that as they learn about the aspects of the topic that are of personal interest, their learning will contribute to the learning of the class as a whole via the team presentations.

2. Selection of Student Teams

Selection of teams will depend on students' interests and the teacher's goals. If the teacher is concerned about questions of race, friendship-based grouping, or heterogeneity, he or she might assign teams.

3. Teambuilding and Skill Development

If teams are assigned heterogeneously, the need for teambuilding will be greater. Structures such as Team Interview, Team Brainstorming, Formations, and Roundrobin can be used to explore the team's interests in the topic, while at the same time developing a bond, a sense of team spirit, among the teammembers.

Team Topic:
Science and technology in New Mexico
Individual Mini-topics:
- Robert Goddard's rocket research
- Development and testing of atomic bomb during Manhattan Project
- Role of New Mexico in Space Shuttle program
- New Mexico as site of Waste Isolation Pilot Project

Team Topic:
Indians of New Mexico
Individual Mini-topics:
- Styles of homes
- Jewelry
- Dress
- Religious ceremonies and dances
- Indians as artists
- Indian tales and legends

Virginia DeBolt: *Write! Cooperative Learning and the Writing Process*

148 Kagan Cooperative Learning • 1 (800) WEE CO-OP

4. Team Topic Selection

For our example, the class topic is the students' state. For the state of New Mexico, some team topic possibilities are: Indians of New Mexico, early Spanish exploration and settlement, the Wild West of Billy the Kid, science and technology, state symbols and what they mean, and state government.

5. Mini-topic Selection

Each team divides its topic into mini-topics, with each individual working on one aspect of the total project. Science and technology in New Mexico, for example, might result in mini-topics about Robert Goddard's rocket research, the development and testing of the atomic bomb during the Manhattan Project, role of New Mexico in the Space Shuttle program, and New Mexico as the site of the Waste Isolation Pilot Project (WIPP). Students researching Indians of New Mexico might develop mini-topics on styles of homes, jewelry or dress, religious ceremonies and dances, Indians as artists, Indian tales and legends.

6. Mini-topic Preparation

Students work individually to research and master their particular mini-topic, with the support of their team. The research may involve library work, interviews, experiments, art work, surveys, map making, individual and class trips, letter writing, watching films or filmstrips, and, most importantly, the careful daily recording of notes, references and information. A special notebook or folder should be designated for this purpose. *During the period of time when the student records the day's learning, encourage them to write with references put away.* That way information will not be copied, but will be processed, organized, and evaluated by the writer as he or she writes.

7. Mini-topic Presentations

Each student presents his or her information to the team. After the presentations, Team Discussions should focus on how the various mini-topics apply to the team topic, ways to relate the information, and any need that might exist for further information or research. The team has become a panel of experts, pulling together individual data into a coherent whole.

8. Preparation of Team Presentations

Teams synthesize the information and plan a way to present it to the class. For the maximum learning, teams must exhibit active synthesis and integration of the mini-topics into a team presentation that becomes more than the sum of its parts. Encourage non-lecture formats for the presentations: skits, learning centers, construction of models or dioramas, demonstrations. Tell students that during the presentation, the classroom belongs to the team presenting. They make arrangements of furniture, determine the use of materials such as the overhead projector, distribute handouts, bring in tape recordings or cooking utensils, set up bulletin boards, or do whatever is necessary to their presentation. Determine a time limit for the presentations and allow teams to practice.

9. Team Presentation

Teams give the presentations. A timekeeper might be appointed. Following each presentation hold a question and answer period. The teacher could lead a feedback session highlighting successful methods of researching and developing the presentations after all the teams have presented.

10. Reflection and Evaluation

Reflection on social skills such as staying on task and equal participation should be an ongoing element of the daily activities of the classroom. There are three types of evaluation in Co-op Co-op. Team presentations are evaluated by the class. The class should develop a group evaluation feedback sheet spotlighting key areas of the presentation; for example, Was it interesting? Were speakers loud and clear? How well did the group work together? The second evaluation is of individual contributions to the team effort. These evaluations are made by teammates. The class should also develop a feedback form for this aspect of the evaluation. Thirdly, each individual hands in a write-up of his or her mini-topic to the teacher. The first two types of evaluation are for appreciation, feedback and growth. The third is for a grade.

References:

Atwell, Nancie, ed. *Coming to Know: Writing to Learn in the Intermediate Grades.* Portsmouth, New Hampshire: Heinemann, 1990.

Kagan, Spencer. *Cooperative Learning.* San Juan Capistrano, California: Kagan Cooperative Learning, 1993.

Virginia DeBolt: *Write! Cooperative Learning and the Writing Process*

150   Kagan Cooperative Learning • 1 (800) WEE CO-OP

Samplings

Cactuses

I always wondered how a cactus survived in the desert. Well when I got eight I knew how a cactus survived because my dad had talked about it several times.

So I am writing a story about it.

Cactuses are very interesting plants. I like the Saguara. The height of the Saguara can get up to 50 feet tall and a diameter of 2½ feet....

Michelle Goeke
Gr. 5 Hillcrest School
Carlsbad, NM
(Note: Michelle made this report into an illustrated pop-up book which she read to the first and second graders.)

Hermit Crabs

Hi my name is Amanda I would like you to meet Hermy he is my pet. I got him last year in Mr. Dodson's class. Mr. Dodson ordered 28 of them and some died. I had 2 hermit crabs but one of my little one died.

Hermit crabs are little crabs that have to stay in shade. The reason they have to stay in shade is becouse they will die if you don't put them in shade.

Hermit crabs eat dog food that is there favorite food. When you give them food you have to mash it up with a hammer or something. They like other kinds of food but they like dogfood the best...

Amanda Brantley
Gr. 5 Hillcrest School
Carlsbad, NM

Virginia DeBolt: *Write! Cooperative Learning and the Writing Process*
Kagan Cooperative Learning • 1 (800) WEE CO-OP

151

Peer Response

Title _____

Name _____

_____

_____

_____

_____

_____

_____

_____

_____

_____

_____

_____

_____

_____

_____

_____

_____

_____

_____

_____

_____

_____

_____

Gambits:

1. You gave really good information about _____

_____

_____.

2. One question I still have is

_____

_____

_____?

Virginia DeBolt: *Write! Cooperative Learning and the Writing Process*

152   Kagan Cooperative Learning • 1 (800) WEE CO-OP

Newspaper Articles & School Newspapers

Man Bites Dog

Lesson-at-a-Glance

Grades	**Academic Skills**	**Time**
3 - 6	• Writing Leads • Writing Headlines	Variable

Materials	**Strand**
• Basic Writing Materials • Index Cards • Handouts	Nonfiction/Reporting

Lesson Overview

In this lesson, students will learn the basics of writing leads and headlines for news articles. Using reproducible cards, the students will form random groups according to the information on the cards. The groups will write headlines and leads with the information.

Students learn two news writing skills in this lesson: using the 5 W's and interviewing. Other lessons in the book, for example, persuasive and editorial writing, are also news writing skills. Poetry and short stories belong in periodicals. Putting all kinds of writing into a regularly published class-

room newspaper serves you and your students as a classbuilder, a communication link with home and community, a writing skill development tool, and a cooperative and social skill builder.

Lesson Sequence

Prewrite
Lead writing with 5 W's using *Find-Someone-Who...*

To give students practice in writing a lead paragraph, prepare five index cards for each of several news stories. If you have 30 students, you need six sets of five cards. You will find suggested labels for the cards on the following pages. At the top of each card you see an identifier, for example, "Ball Game." Under the identifier is printed one of the 5 W's needed in a lead paragraph. Each card tells only one piece of informa-

Structures

• *Class Discussion*
• *Find-Someone-Who...*
• *Guess-The-Fib*
• *Independent Writing*
• *Mix-Freeze-Pair*
• *Roundrobin*
• *Roundtable*
• *Team Collaboration*
• *Team Discussion*

tion, either who, what, where, when, or why (sometimes how). The "where" card might read: Ball Game. Boys' and Girls' Club Gym. The "what" card might read: Ball Game. Elementary League Basketball Tournament. Mix up the cards and distribute one to each student. Students move around the room searching for others who have information needed to complete their lead paragraph.

Write

Headlines and lead paragraphs using *Team Discussion*

After the students have located classmates holding bits of information on matching topics, have these five children sit together to work as a team on this lesson. Teams display the five index cards where they can be seen. Each teammember writes a headline and a lead paragraph from the information on the 5W cards.

Confer

Rewrite a team lead paragraph using *Team Collaboration*

Teammembers read aloud in a Round-robin. Teammembers discuss various approaches to writing the headline and the lead. They collaborate on rewriting the five W's into one "best possible" headline and lead paragraph. A Recorder writes the team's paragraph.

Proof/Edit

Editing Conference using *Roundtable*

Pass the paragraph around the table for editing and proofreading by team members.

Publish

Discuss supporting details using *Class Discussion*

In a class discussion have each team share the headline and lead they collaborated to write. Talk about additional information, or details, that the story needs in order to be complete. In the ball game example, details about teams involved, elementary schools represented, grade levels of the players, and team standings might be mentioned. Have students suggest ways the details could be added to create complete news articles.

Lesson Extension

Teambuilding news article using *Guess-the-Fib*

If you change team composition each six weeks, Guess-the-Fib provides writers with fascinating facts about their new teammates to write in a news article. In Guess-The-Fib, students state two true facts and one fib about themselves. Teammates come to consensus as to which statement they think is the fib. If they guess wrong, they try again. Continue until every team member has given facts and fib.

Alternative Activities

Prewrite

Find an interview partner using *Mix-Freeze-Pair*

Have students wander throughout the room until previous teams are completely mixed. Call out, "Freeze!" Students pair up with someone standing nearby. This pair will interview each other for the purpose of writing news articles about each other. Allow five minutes for each interview, or ten minutes for the pair. This activity is a good classbuilder.

Confer

Share interview articles using *Roundrobin*

Each pair should join with another pair to make Roundrobin groups of four students. During the Roundrobin, students read the articles aloud. After every student read his or her writing, include some form of feedback. Feedback might be praisers for the writer, additional questions for the interviewee, or suggestions on revisions from the interviewee to the writer.

A School Newspaper

Writing, assembling, and publishing a newspaper is a group project that fits easily into structures such as Co-op Co-op and Jigsaw. A newspaper contains all kinds of writing: reviews, editorials, jokes, recipes, poems, announcements, ads, and articles reporting on newsworthy events and people.

With photocopying technology, producing a school newspaper is not the daunting task it formerly was. It would be helpful, but not absolutely necessary, to have computer software capable of word processing, large fonts for headlines, clip art, and possibly column layouts. Select user-friendly software that the students can use. With cutting and pasting, a combination of software such as Print Shop and Bank Street Writer or MECC Writer would work well. Photocopiers being the handy dandy items that they are, you could print a newspaper made of the actual handwritten and illustrated work the reporters turn in. Enlarging, reducing, snipping - layout's done.

A camera is desirable. A word of advise, however, about photocopying snapshots: be sure faces are well lighted, keep the background colors light, and keep most subjects within about six feet of the photographer.

Time is a variable, depending on frequency of publication, newspaper size, and the amount of help you have. Time might be scheduled before or after school for meetings with a newspaper staff or newspaper club if your entire school participates.

W... Egg Drop
Any student in the school

W... Egg Drop
Design a container that will keep an uncooked egg from breaking when dropped off the school roof.

W... Egg Drop
Friday afternoon immediately after the last lunch recess.

W... Egg Drop
Students meet on the primary playground.

W.., Egg Drop
Ms. Ebbetts will take the eggs to the roof; Ms. Groves will be in charge of dropping the eggs.

W... Field Trip
All fifth grade classes

W... Field Trip
Bus trip

W... Field Trip
Friday, April 22, from 8:30 a.m. until 3:00 p.m.

W... Field Trip
To state park

W... Field Trip
Ranger will explain the ecosystem and lead Project Wild games.

5 W's
Reproducible

Directions: Write each label on a separate index card or reproduce these and cut them up. Each set has five cards. Make as many sets as you need for your class.

Each box holds the 5 W's necessary for a lead paragraph. The five components in each box must be cut apart and distributed randomly around the classroom. Tell students, "Walk around the room searching for someone who has information on your topic. You should be in groups of five when you find everyone."

W... Ball Game
Elementary League Basketball Tournament

W... Ball Game
Boys' and Girls' Club Gyms

W... Ball Game
Saturday, November 10 and Sunday, November 11 beginning at 1:00 p.m.

W... Ball Game
Players from every elementary school in the city.

W... Ball Game
Team trophies and championship trophies will be awarded.

Virginia DeBolt: *Write! Cooperative Learning and the Writing Process*

156   Kagan Cooperative Learning • 1 (800) WEE CO-OP

5 W's
Reproducible

W... Science Fair
Exhibit of science projects

W... Science Fair
For grades 5-12

W... Science Fair
At the high school gym

W... Science Fair
Friday through Sunday, February 3-5

W... Science Fair
To demonstrate science experiments and achievements.

W... World Fair
Booths displaying food, clothing, pictures, and more from countries all over the world.

W... World Fair
In the school multi-purpose room

W... World Fair
Mrs. Apodaca's sixth graders will be in their booths to share information and answer questions.

W... World Fair
Monday and Tuesday of next week. Tuesday night is Parents' Night.

W... World Fair
Every class will have a turn touring the World's Fair.

W... Program
First graders from Mr. Gutierrez's class

W... Program
"Holiday Magic" Christmas songs and skits

W... Program
December 14 at 7:00 p.m.

W... Program
In the school multi-purpose room

W... Program
All parents, friends, and students are invited.

The 5 W'S of Lead Paragraphs

Name_____Date_____

A news article tells all the important facts as soon as possible. Those facts tell Who, What, When, Where, Why, and sometimes How. Use this page to make sure you have all the important information for a news article.

WHO is this article about?_____

WHAT is happening?_____

WHERE will it take place?_____

WHEN will it happen?_____

WHY is this happening?_____

HOW will this happen?_____

What additional information and detail might I add?_____

_____

_____

_____

Samplings

I'd like to introduce my new friend Andrew. His favorit color is Green. If he was a car he would be a 5.0. If he were a city he would be carlsbad. He said iff he had another name it would be Chris. If he were a teacher he would teach at Hillcrest school. If he were a book he would be a Dictionry

Dustin Rauch
Gr. 4 Hillcrest School
Carlsbad, NM

I survaid My 4th grade Class to see why people should help other people And this is what they saied

Mrs. Debolt the 4th grade teacher has a sloagan "May God grant you double what you wish for me"
Melissa Wade is a 4th grader and she says "Other people should help other people because is they didn't the world would proubaly be gone"....

Kristin Johnson
Gr. 4 Hillcrest School
Carlsbad, NM

Virginia DeBolt: *Write! Cooperative Learning and the Writing Process*
Kagan Cooperative Learning • 1 (800) WEE CO-OP

159

Newspaper Articles & School Newspapers

Peer Response

Title _____

Name _____

_____

_____

_____

_____

_____

_____

_____

_____

_____

_____

_____

_____

_____

_____

_____

_____

_____

_____

_____

_____

_____

_____

_____

_____

_____

_____

Gambits:

1. Your lead was clear because _____
_____
_____.

2. The best thing about the headline was _____
_____
_____

Virginia DeBolt: *Write! Cooperative Learning and the Writing Process*

160   Kagan Cooperative Learning • 1 (800) WEE CO-OP

Biographies

Celebration of Life

Lesson-at-a-Glance

Grades	Academic Skills	Time
3 - 6	• Planning and conducting an interview • Writing & illustrating a biography	1 - 2 weeks

Materials		Strand
• Basic writing materials • Tape recorders • Party supplies	• Book binding materials • Camera, film or art supplies for illustrating	Nonfiction/Reporting

Lesson Overview

In this lesson, the student will write the biography of a person the student knows. The student will practice interviewing skills before interviewing the subject of the biography. The subjects of the biographies will be invited to the classroom for a celebration and Read-In.

Announce to the students that it is "Biography Week." They will interview an older person in their family. (Other interview sources: business people in the school's neighborhood, school staff, family friends, local officials). The biography will be based on what they learn in the interview. Explain the resources you have that they might use to tape or photograph the interviewee. Two photos or illustrations of each subject are required since students will make two copies of the biography: one for the subject and one for the writer. Tell the class that at the end of the writing the biographies will be shared at a Read-In party. They may wish to select someone as their subject who is able to come to school during the day.

Lesson Sequence

Prewrite Interview preparation using *Team Interview*

Give students a time to select a subject and to contact the subject for an appointment. Use Team Interview to develop a set of questions to ask during the talk with the subject of the biography. During Team Interview each student in turn stands and

---

- • *Experts Edit*
- • *Individual Interviews*
- • *Independent Writing*
- • *Read In*
- • *Teams Confer*
- • *Team Interview*

Structures

Virginia DeBolt: *Write! Cooperative Learning and the Writing Process*
Kagan Cooperative Learning • 1 (800) WEE CO-OP

161

announces who he or she will be writing about. Reasons for picking that particular person should be explained. Teammates ask questions about the person whose life story will be told. The student hearing the questions notes the ideas and topics about which his or her teammates are curious.

Encourage authors to tailor their questions to the individual involved. Someone writing about her grandfather who grew up in a village in Mexico would not want the same list of questions as another student writing about an aunt who operates heavy machinery for a construction company. After each team member has a list of questions garnered from teammates, allow time for the questions to be added to, organized, and rewritten with ample space for answers.

Gather Information using *Individual Interviews*

Students need time to meet with interviewees. Biography subjects could be invited to school for the interviews. That would simplify taping and photographing difficulties students might have away from school. Other subjects might prefer to be interviewed at home.

Write

Write biography using *Independent Writing*

Students prepare a draft of their subject's life based on what they learned from the interview.

Confer

Confer on content using *Team Confer*

Using a Roundrobin approach, students share their first drafts with teammates. Have team members concentrate on the usual issues of order, effective beginning, and clarity. Provide time for revising.

Proof/Edit

Editing Conference using *Experts Edit*

Pick four or eight expert proofreaders and editors and provide them with work areas in the four corners of the room. As students complete the revised draft, they seek help with editing from one of the experts.

The subjects of the biographies might appreciate an opportunity to edit content.

Publish

Authors and subjects celebrate using *Read-In*

Make two copies of each biography (one for the author, one for the subject) and bind them into books. By written invitation, invite the subjects of the books, as well as other interested individuals, to a Read-In. Other interested parties might include the local newspaper reporter/photographer. Celebrate with some good P.R. for your school. Wouldn't this be a nice multicultural celebration for American Education Week?

During the Read-In pass the books around the room from team to team so that the children and guests can read every book. Conclude with a party honoring the authors and the contributions of the people about whom they wrote. Pass the cookies, please.

Virginia DeBolt: *Write! Cooperative Learning and the Writing Process*

162   Kagan Cooperative Learning • 1 (800) WEE CO-OP

Samplings

My Great-Grandma Diane yawned + stepped out of the old car.

"Wake-up! We're here!" said Johnny to Bill. Bill was the sleepy kind it seemed like World War II couldn't wake him up.

"Okay, Okay, I am awake," Bill complained. As all of them were walking into the yard a large squirl ran down a tree.

Out came Grandma. After having a talk they stepped in to the old car again...

Michelle Goeke
Gr. 5 Hillcrest School
Carlsbad, NM

Virginia DeBolt: *Write! Cooperative Learning and the Writing Process*
Kagan Cooperative Learning • 1 (800) WEE CO-OP

163

Biographies

Peer Response

Title _____

Name _____

Gambits:

1. When you told _____
about your subject, it was
_____
_____.

2. Your quotes are _____
_____
_____.

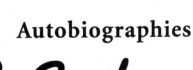

Subject Matters

Lesson-at-a-Glance

Grades	**Academic Skills**	**Time**
3 - 6	Writing autobiography related to a single curriculum topic	2 -3 lessons

Materials		**Strand**
• Basic writing materials • Carbon paper	• Pictures of each student • Subject Matters Timeline Reproducible	Nonfiction/Reporting

Lesson Overview

In this lesson, the student will write a learner's autobiography. The autobiography will describe the learner's growth in a particular school subject, such as math. The autobiography, coupled with a picture of the learner, will be displayed in the classroom.

Lesson Sequence

Prewrite

Personal reflection using
Think-Pair-Share

Tell students that they will be writing their autobiography. It will be a special kind of autobiography because it will tell the story of their life experiences with a particular school subject. Students might write "My Math Autobiography," or, "My Computer Autobiography," or, "My Reading Autobiography," for example.

Ask them to think of the subject in school about which they want to write. Then ask students to pair up and share their ideas. During the sharing time, students need to be specific about incidents and insights in their lives as readers or mathematicians or artists. Kids could get into big time metacognition here, writing down reflective insights into learning processes!

Timeline talk using
Pair Discussion

Reproduce the Subject Matters Timeline on the following page for each student. Pairs discuss the information collected during the Think-Pair-Share. They decide how the information can be recorded and organized on the time line. The timeline will be

---

Structures

* **Think-Pair-Share**
* **Free Write**
* **Independent Writing**
* **Roundrobin**
* **One Stray**
* **Roam the Room**
* **Pair Discussion**

Virginia DeBolt: *Write! Cooperative Learning and the Writing Process*
Kagan Cooperative Learning • 1 (800) WEE CO-OP

165

a handy outline of learning experiences for writers to use during the Independent Writing time.

Write

Write autobiography using *Independent Writing*

The children work independently to write the autobiography.

Confer

Confer on content using *Roundrobin*

In teams, the students take turns reading their first drafts aloud. The three listening offer praise, pose questions, and make suggestions. Continue until each team member has shared his or her rough draft. Give time for individual work on revisions.

Proof/Edit

Roundtable editing using *One Stray*

With carbon paper or the photocopier, each student readies three copies of the revised first draft. Have the number one member of each team stand and move to the next team, taking the three copies of the work needing proofreading. After listening to number one read the story aloud, three teammates from the new group edit and proof.

Since the members of each new team are not familiar with the content of the writing from the conference on content, they can approach the work with fresh eyes. After three who stayed have individually edited and proofread for the one who strayed, they should briefly confer to check for agreement. Then one's return home. Two's stand and move two teams away for editing and proofreading. Continue with the number

three and four team members, or until each team member has "strayed" for editing help. After all writers are back in their desks, allow time for revision and rewriting.

Publish

Celebrate authors using *Roam the Room*

The final draft, complete with a picture of the author, can be hung in the hall or on a bulletin board.

Lesson Extensions

Your Book of Life

Gather up a collection of autobiographical information, beginning with the Subject Matters story, and have each student make a book. Include some or all of the following:

1. A family tree
2. A story the student writes about his/her great-grandparents after interviewing his/her parents about what it was like for them when they went to visit at their grandparents.
3. Personal artifact stories (see p. 91)
4. A history of the family name
5. A time capsule piece called "My Life and Times"
6. A self portrait
7. A bio-poem

Alternative Activities

Prewrite

Tap into personal memories using
Free Write

There are no rules in Free Write, no mechanics questions, no spelling worries. Free Write is solo brainstorming. Tell students to write everything they can remember about themselves and their chosen subject area. As with brainstorming, the purpose is to get down as much as possible quickly, and leave evaluating until later.

Virginia DeBolt: *Write! Cooperative Learning and the Writing Process*
Kagan Cooperative Learning • 1 (800) WEE CO-OP

167

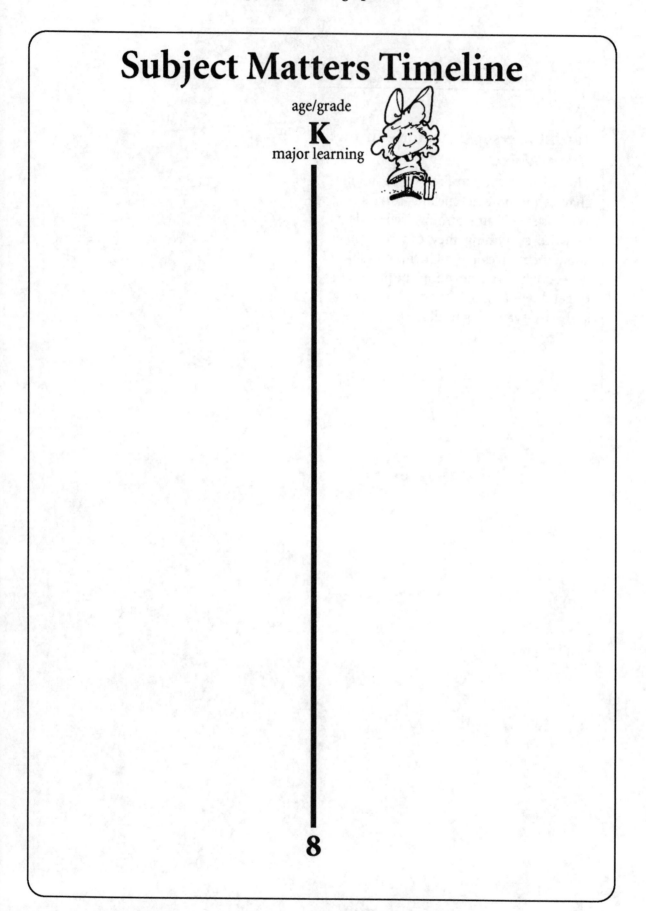

Subject Matters Timeline

age/grade

K

major learning

8

Virginia DeBolt: *Write! Cooperative Learning and the Writing Process*

Kagan Cooperative Learning • 1 (800) WEE CO-OP

168

Samplings

My Art Autobiography

When I was in preschool I liked to color. My favoriote colors were pink, purple, and blue. In kindergarden I liked to glue things, but I liked paste better than glue. In third grade I made a reindeer puppet out of paper. Last year I did a fire prevetion poster and that was fun. And we mde pottery for our moms out of clay. Then we made igloos out of sugar cubes and icing. This year I learned how to make piniata's, that was neat. We did a play and I got to draw the characters. They were a blue hary moster and two little girls. The last thing we did was a save the Earth poster. When I get home from school I like to draw. And in the summer I watch secret city. It's a show on T.V. that shows you how to draw. All this made my favorite subject, art.

Casey Williams
Gr. 5 Hillcrest Elementary
Carlsbad, NM

My Spelling Autobiography

In preschool I learned the sounds ā, ă, ē, ĕ, ī, ĭ, ō, ŏ, ū, and ŭ. By kindergarten I learned the 1 syllable words pat, sat, hat, tip, hop, flip, fall, call, mud, dud, and glad. First grade I started on two syllable words like started, happy, spelling, and story. In second grade I advanced to encyclopedia, detective, and dictionary. In third grade I started spelling words like tight, though, through, and thought. In fourth grade we started spelling countries like Yugoslavia and Indonesia. In fifth grade we started vocabulary and definitions.

Vicky Vargas
Gr. 5 Hillcrest Elementary
Carlsbad, NM

My Math Autobiography

I learned my numbers in Kindergarden. We played games with numbers and it was fun. Dot-To-Dots was my favorite game in Kindergarden. In First-Grade we learned how to add little easy numbers on our fingers. I loved to add those numbers. We also learned to subtract the easy numbers too. In second-Grade we learned how to add and subtract harder numbers. In Third-Grade I learned how to multiply easy numbrers and I learned how to divide easy numbers. In Fourth-Grade I learned about fractions and mopre about multiplying and dividing. I am now in Fifth-Grade and I am learning lots more about fractions. I am still learning more about dividing and multiplying. We are learning about measurement too.

Katrina Gutierrez
Gr. 5 Hillcrest Elementary
Carlsbad, NM

Autobiographies

Peer Response

Title _____

Name _____

_____

_____

_____

_____

_____

_____

_____

_____

_____

_____

_____

_____

_____

_____

_____

_____

_____

_____

_____

_____

_____

_____

_____

_____

_____

_____

_____

_____

Gambits:

1. I understood your feelings when you said _____

_____

_____ .

2. Could you tell me a little more about the way you first learned _____

_____

_____ ?

Virginia DeBolt: *Write! Cooperative Learning and the Writing Process*

170   Kagan Cooperative Learning • 1 (800) WEE CO-OP

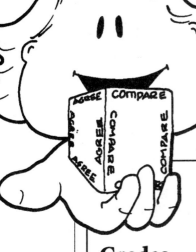

Taking Sides

Lesson-at-a-Glance

Grades	Academic Skills	Time
3 - 6	Supporting a position with reasons	1 - 3 sessions

Materials
- Basic writing materials
- Cubing Reproducible
- Scissors and glue
- Teacher-prepared question on current issue

Strand
Opinion Making

Lesson Overview

In this lesson, the student will examine a controversy using a Cube-It reproducible. The student will write an editorial stating his or her opinion on the problem.

Lesson Sequence

Prewrite

Examine a problem using *Cube-It Brainstorming*

Have student pairs cut out and glue the Cube (page 177). The teacher poses a question or presents an issue taken from current events. Pick something a bit controversial, a bit open to expressing strong opinions. Our society flourishes on controversial questions

— just be careful not to ask about the ones that might get you fired! Students will have strong opinions about school policy or school environment, always a good source of editorial issues. Working with the Cube in pairs, students look at the problem from six different sides, generating as many ideas as possible. Students make note of ideas, or list ideas as they develop during the cubing process.

Write

Write an editorial using *Independent Writing*

Each child works independently to write an editorial.

Confer

Confer on content using *Teams Consult*

Develop gambits with the class that are effective in critiquing an editorial, such as

- *Cube-It Brainstorm*
- *Roundrobin*
- *Pairs Compare*
- *Independent Writing*
- *Teams Consult*
- *Roundtable*
- *Rotating Feedback*

Structures

"Your most convincing point is... Did you consider . . . ?" Put two teams together in a writing conference group. Using two teams in the conference will give fresh insight into the positions that were developed during prewriting. Have students read the editorials aloud and work together to strengthen content. Then students return to desks for revising.

Proof/Edit

Editing conference using
Roundtable

Within teams, students pass their revised copies around for editing and proofreading by their teammates. Work then begins on preparation of the final copy.

Publish

Celebrate authors using
Rotating Feedback

Post all the editorials. You may want to include a blank feedback sheet for readers to use in offering praise and appreciation. Students move about the room reading the work of other writers. If your school has a newspaper, have students publish the editorials there.

Alternative Activities

Prewrite

Take a stand using
Roundrobin

After they have thoroughly examined an issue, say to students, "Think about your ideas on this issue based on what you've talked about during the Cubing. Go around your team in a Roundrobin and explain exactly where you stand."

Evaluate ideas using
Pairs Compare

Between nearby teams, student pairs share ideas gathered during the brainstorming and Roundrobin. While comparing and discussing each other's ideas, have students evaluate and analyze the ideas. When finished, each individual is prepared to take a stand and list reasons supporting it.

Reference

Hill, Susan and Tim. *The Collaborative Classroom: A Guide to Cooperative Learning.* Heinemann Educational Books, 1990.

Virginia DeBolt: *Write! Cooperative Learning and the Writing Process*

172   Kagan Cooperative Learning • 1 (800) WEE CO-OP

Editorial Cubing

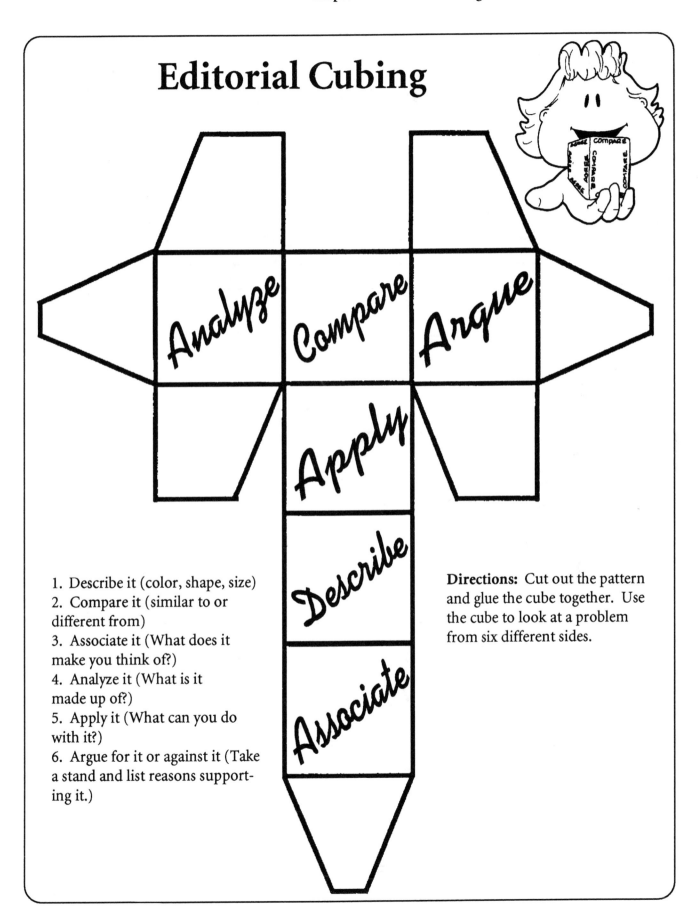

1. Describe it (color, shape, size)
2. Compare it (similar to or different from)
3. Associate it (What does it make you think of?)
4. Analyze it (What is it made up of?)
5. Apply it (What can you do with it?)
6. Argue for it or against it (Take a stand and list reasons supporting it.)

Directions: Cut out the pattern and glue the cube together. Use the cube to look at a problem from six different sides.

Editorial Cubing

Record your ideas here...

Virginia DeBolt: *Write! Cooperative Learning and the Writing Process*

Kagan Cooperative Learning • 1 (800) WEE CO-OP

174

Samplings

Dogs in the pound

I don't wan't dog's or cats in the pound that are going to die. I wish they would keep the dogs and cats untill someone buys them expecilly the cuite and furry ones. Dogs and cats should be free from dieing. If a dog or cat gets put in the pound for no resson the person should be locked up for a month or two. That is crulltee. But I love animals. Just because a dog kills something for food don't put the dog to sleep. spanke it. Don't be mean to dogs or cats. Be nice to them, keep then alive.

Kristin Johnson
Gr. 4 Hillcrest School
Carlsbad, NM

Why the earth is round
I think the earth should be square or, Rectangle, triangle, or OUal. If it were square you could walk to the edge of the earth and throw trash In to outer space and the black hole would eat it up. A square earth would be better. It would be sunny all the time and the plants would grow as tall as trees.

Robert Vargas
Gr. 4 Hillcrest School
Carlsbad, NM

Opinion's to be Shared
The disabled or handicapped should be treated like any other person, They are somebody too. Not just a doll. There are many people not being treated right and som of them arnt hurt or nothing is wrong with them They are just fine you got to look for whats inside of them not whats out side. They should be treated equilly too !!!!

Michelle Goeke
Gr. 5 Hillcrest School
Carlsbad, NM

My Opinion

Should children be spanked for bad behavior? Let's talk to Gloria Patterson.

"I think children should be spanked if they are not behaving, but if they are behaving you shouldn't spank them just for fun. That's all I have to say.

Gloria Patterson
Gr. 4 Hillcrest School
Carlsbad, NM

Editorial Writing

Peer Response

Title

Name

Gambits:

1. Your opinion is that ____

____

____.

2. Your best points are ____

____

____

Speeches

I Have a Dream

Lesson-at-a-Glance

Grades	Academic Skills	Time
3 - 6	Writing and delivering a speech	2 - 3 lessons

Materials	Strand
• Basic writing materials • Microphones • Loudspeakers	Opinion Making

Lesson Overview

In this lesson, the student will write a speech. With the help of a partner, the student will practice the speech before delivering it to an audience.

Since it is probable that speech writing would be needed by only one or a few students at any given time, all the structures in this lesson are planned for pairs. This way, the structures will hold from one to thirty speech writers.

• *Independent Writing*
• *Pair Discussion*
• *Pairs Confer*
• *Pairs Edit*
• *Pairs Rehearse*
• *Think-Write-Pair-Share*

Structures

Lesson Sequence

Prewrite

Plan a speech using *Think-Write-Pair-Share*

Why speak? About what? To whom? Have students

reflect on the purpose of the public speech. (Is it for a student council election, to introduce skits during a class program, to read over the school public address system during morning announcements?)

As students reflect, they should be jotting down thoughts about the content necessary for the speech. Allow two or three minutes of think-write time. Students pair up and share ideas. Following the sharing time, students may have new ideas to add to their notes on content.

Audience is important to consider — will it be parents, classmates, the whole student body?

Write

Write a Speech using *Independent Writing*

Each student works independently on his or her speech.

Confer

Confer on content using
Pairs Confer

Pairs read the speeches aloud. The conference should address questions of content and audience. Is the meaning clear and effective? Will it hold the listeners' interest?

Each student makes any necessary revisions. The Pairs Conference might be repeated two or three times, until the content of the speech is well polished and effective.

Proof/Edit

Editing conference using
Pairs Edit

The speechmaker, along with his/her helper, examines the revised draft for spelling and punctuation. Have students pay close attention to punctuation as an aid to meaning for the oral reader.

Oral Interpretation Marks:

Speakers can insert marks and signs into the text of a speech to help improve delivery. Arrows (↗)can remind the speaker to look up at the audience. Go beyond normal punctuation with big reminders written as stage directions. (PAUSE) (SMILE)

Publish

Practice a speech using
Pairs Rehearse

Before actually delivering his or her speech, the youngster should have rehearsal time using the microphone or other devices. The partner helper is there to critique points such as volume, rate of speaking, voice clarity, and body language.

Deliver a Speech

The student delivers his or her speech before the intended audience. (PAUSE FOR APPLAUSE.)

Alternative Activities

Prewrite

Role play using
Pair Discussion

Using the notes and plans, each student works orally at role playing possibilities for the speech. He or she can try out different approaches and wordings with a partner to help decide what works best. Let pairs continue until a speech is ready to pop from the pencil when they sit down to write.

Speeches

Peer Response

Title _____

Name _____

_____
_____
_____
_____
_____
_____
_____
_____
_____
_____
_____
_____
_____
_____
_____
_____
_____
_____
_____
_____
_____
_____
_____
_____
_____

Gambits:

1. You are clear and interesting in the part where _____
_____
_____.

2. The tone of your voice is
_____
_____
_____.

Make your Point

Lesson-at-a-Glance

Grades	**Academic Skills**	**Time**
3 - 6	• Write persuasive paragraphs • Use main idea sentence • Use summary sentence (grades 4-6)	1 - 3 sessions

Materials	**Strand**
• Basic writing materials • Value Line Strips	Opinion Making

- *Class Value Lines*
- *Think-Write-Pair-Share*
- *Independent Writing*
- *Pairs Confer*

Structures

Lesson Overview

In this lesson, the student will take a position of agreement or disagreement with a controversial statement. The student will work to sharpen his or her point of view. The student will write a composition stating his or her position and offering reasons to support his or her thinking.

Children know how to be persuasive. By age two, they can persuade Mom to hand over a cookie. By age 16, many kids are so good at persuasion that Mom and Dad hand over a car. They've probably figured out their friends (and their teachers!) with the same accuracy. Here's their chance to apply a lifetime of learning to their writing.

Lesson Sequence

Prewrite

Take a position using *Class Value Line*

Have the materials monitor give each team member a value line strip. The teacher makes a statement requiring a value judgment. Write it on the board, too. Some examples are: "Spanking should be used in school to control students' behavior," or, "Women are as effective in combat as men," or, "We should do away with movie ratings," or, "We need five minutes longer in the cafeteria at lunchtime." On the count of three, each individual marks the value line strip to indicate strong agreement, strong disagreement, or something in between.

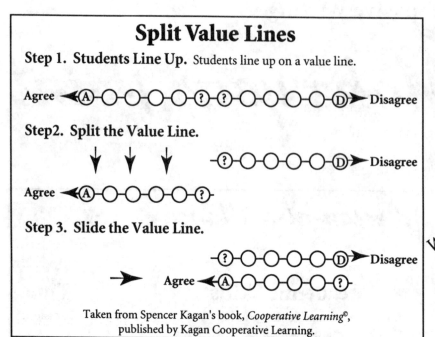

Split Value Lines

Step 1. Students Line Up. Students line up on a value line.

Agree ← Ⓐ—○—○—○—○—?—?—○—○—○—○—Ⓓ → Disagree

Step2. Split the Value Line.

↓ ↓ ↓   ?—○—○—○—○—Ⓓ → Disagree

Agree ← Ⓐ—○—○—○—○—?

Step 3. Slide the Value Line.

                ?—○—○—○—○—Ⓓ → Disagree

→   Agree ← Ⓐ—○—○—○—○—?

Taken from Spencer Kagan's book, *Cooperative Learning©*,
published by Kagan Cooperative Learning.

Students literally "take a stand" on an imaginary value line stretching from one side of the room to the other. The spot where the student stands corresponds with the spot he or she marked on the value line strip. Split the value line in the middle. Have the children slide the halves of the line so that the person on the end who agrees most strongly is facing someone from the middle who either has no strong opinion or can see both sides of the issue. (See illustration.) The student who disagrees most strongly will also be facing a person from the middle of the line.

The teacher picks one of the two facing lines to speak first. Students simultaneously explain their positions to the classmate opposite. Before the facing student may answer, he or she must paraphrase the statement made by the first speaker. After the second student speaks, the first student must paraphrase.

Follow the paraphrasing with a two or three minute challenge/persuade discussion time. The challenge/persuade discussion time is critical to the student's final position. During the discussion students sharpen arguments, find reasons to maintain or change their position, and select the best points in favor of their position.

Write Write to persuade using *Independent Writing*

Before beginning to write, students must make a decision. Who is the audience for this persuasive writing? If the school principal is the intended audience, perhaps it should be written in letter format. If the school newspaper will publish it, an editorial might be appropriate. If it will be read by classmates, perhaps the standard paragraph format is what is needed.

Students work on a first draft. Suggest that paragraphs begin with a main idea and proceed from the least powerful to the most powerful argument. Depending on grade level, a summary sentence might end the writing.

Confer Confer on content using *Pairs Confer*

Students work in pairs. Now, students stop arguing a point of view to become helpers in a revision conference. Is the content clear? Are the points made in the best order? What could the writer do to improve weak arguments? After Pairs Confer, students revise their first draft.

Virginia DeBolt: *Write! Cooperative Learning and the Writing Process*

182   Kagan Cooperative Learning • 1 (800) WEE CO-OP

Proof/Edit

Editing conference using *Pairs Confer*

Pairs Confer again to edit and proofread. Depending on who will be the audience for the persuasive writing, the student might request an editing conference with the teacher. Error-free copy persuades. Copy full of mistakes only makes the reader wonder if the author knows what he is talking about. A final draft is written.

Publish

Students deliver the paragraphs to the intended audience.

Alternative Activities

Prewrite

Main idea sentences using *Think-Write-Pair-Share*

The teacher says, "Think about a good main idea sentence for your paragraph." Allow a bit of Think time, then say, "Write your sentence on a slip of paper." Have the students pair up and read the sentences aloud. Invite some to share with the class. Talk about what makes a good main idea sentence. If the first sentences shared are like this: "I disagree that we should not rate movies," the teacher needs to help students find better ways of stating their position and do another round of Think-Write-Pair-Share.

Virginia DeBolt: *Write! Cooperative Learning and the Writing Process*

Kagan Cooperative Learning • 1 (800) WEE CO-OP   183

Reproducible Value Line Strips

Primary

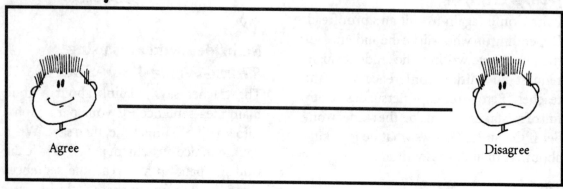

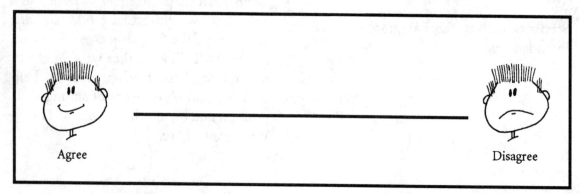

Intermediate

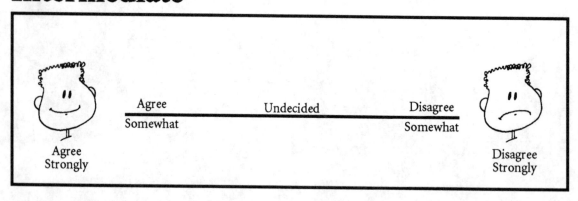

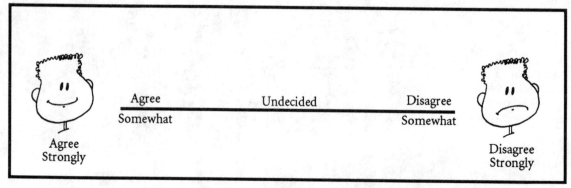

Virginia DeBolt: *Write! Cooperative Learning and the Writing Process*

184 Kagan Cooperative Learning • 1 (800) WEE CO-OP

Samplings

Making Bad Judgements

Kids should not be spanked because of something they did. I think that parents shouldn't be mat at a kid for doing something they didn't know they couldn't do.

Now if a kid does something and knokws he or she shouldn't have done, the kid should be spanked. My point is a kid shouldn't be spanked because of something they didn't know they couldt do.

Rusty Edmondson
Gr. 5 Hillcrest School
Carlsbad, NM

CHILDREN AND DISCIPLIN {GO TOGETHER}

I think children can be controlled by disciplinary spanking.

Because I see children who have never been raised under disciplin in there intire life. Because of this, their behavior is terrible.

And I see children who have been raised under disciplin and their behavior is pretty good. Now I'm not saying children who have been disciplined are little angles. But I am say that children who have are better to get along with than undisciplined children.

Children who haven't been raised under disciplin are raised thinking everything is okay. and they have no respect for right and wrong. And children who have been raised under disciplin know that not everything is okay and they have respect for right and wrong ...

Michael Tackitt
Gr. 5 Hillcrest School
Carlsbad, NM

Spanking is not Acceptable

Children should not be spanked because it could harm us kids. It will just make us wost. Spanking making us cry and our parents don't know how it feels. They don't feel the pain and suffering. It just makes us feel unwelcomed and makes us run away. But my strongest point is that we will be like our parents and hit our children.

Adrian Garcia
Gr. 5 Hillcrest School
Carlsbad, NM

Virginia DeBolt: *Write! Cooperative Learning and the Writing Process*
Kagan Cooperative Learning • 1 (800) WEE CO-OP

185

Persuasive Writing

Title

Name

Gambits:

1. Your strongest points are

_____

_____.

2. Could you say something

to persuade me that _____

_____

_____?

Virginia DeBolt: *Write! Cooperative Learning and the Writing Process*

Kagan Cooperative Learning • 1 (800) WEE CO-OP

Responding to Literature

Language is the glue connecting writing, reading, listening and speaking. The separation of writing and reading is an artificial one. The teacher who bridges the gaps between writing and other aspects of language helps children become lifelong writers and readers. Students cross that bridge when the classroom is filled with many opportunities to read and respond in writing to good literature.

The following suggestions for responding to literature are merely a beginning, a springboard, for your imagination as teacher.

Daily Storytime

Even in upper grades, it is important for the teacher to read aloud to the students every day during a regular story time. Hearing a story read well provides a model of language students can get from no other source. It also gives students a shared experience about which to talk and write. Have students respond occasionally to the story in their Learner's Journal, a reading response notebook, or a writer's notebook.

Writing/Reading Retreat

Schedule an overnight retreat devoted to writing, reading, sharing stories and listening to stories. Hold it in the gym, a church, or a Boy Scout campground. Get plenty of help from parents and other teachers, so that you can lead varied activities devoted to silent reading, shared oral stories, writing about literature, writing about shared retreat experiences, and oral reading of many kinds of books.

Have students keep a special retreat notebook for ideas and thoughts they find interesting in the reading and sharing, connections they may make to their lives or to other reading, unforgettable moments, details and observations, words or phrases, comments about the food, the sleeping accommodations, and everything else. Such a retreat notebook will be fertile ground for writing ideas throughout the remainder of the year.

Mystery Author

Give students a paragraph or two from a short literature selection. Challenge them to write the ending paragraph of the story. Then, working in teams of four, students select or combine their paragraphs into a single paragraph they consider a good ending for the story. The group paragraphs are collected by the teacher. He or she types them, correcting spelling and mechanical errors. He or she also types the ending written by the real author.

Next day, give the real ending and the new endings to the teams and ask them to pick they one they think is the real ending. (They must not reveal which ending is the one written by their team.) As teams announce their choices, they must give supporting arguments for their position.

Students may support choices with comments about tone, point of view, language choice, sentence length, and writing style, although they may not have labels for such ideas. After revealing the "real" author, the teacher can pin the labels on the new concepts of writing style the students discovered while playing detective.

Connections

Read or reproduce a small section from a text. Have students record thoughts that went through their minds as it was read. Such connections might lead to writing

Text	Connections
————	————
————	————
————	————
————	————

projects for the students. The two column format shown is nice for this.

Literature Demonstrations

Make a transparency of a sample of professional writing with which the class is familiar, and project it on the overhead. Help the children notice how the professionals use punctuation marks, nouns, verbs or other mechanics. Talk about what might be misunderstood if the mechanics were not used properly.

Read-Quad-Respond

Kagan Cooperative Learning publishes a book on Cooperative Learning and Critical Thinking by Chuck Wiederhold called *The Question Matrix*. A packet of manipulatives can be purchased to accompany the book. Using the Question Matrix, or Q-Matrix, students pose questions of their own making. Wiederhold's book includes several language arts lessons describing the process.

I suggest that you read a selection aloud to the class — something wonderful but brief enough to complete in one sitting — perhaps something by Byrd Baylor or Crescent Dragonwagon. Use four sheets of paper for each student, and the four quadrant cards from the *Q-Materials Packet*. Have students head each sheet with a question about the story, created from each of the four quadrant cards. Then give the students five minutes per sheet to write an answer to their questions. After responding to all four questions, the students arrange their responses in a way that makes sense. Finish with oral sharing, in pairs, teams, or as a whole class discussion.

Virginia DeBolt: *Write! Cooperative Learning and the Writing Process*
Kagan Cooperative Learning • 1 (800) WEE CO-OP

188

One Quad Layering

Begin by reading literature aloud to the class. Murray (1990) describes layering as writing about something, then starting on a new page and writing about it again without reading the first page. Then do it a third time, a fourth, or more. Layering with question prompts from only one quadrant of the Q-Matrix would be an interesting writing experience, particularly using the quadrant asking for speculation, probabilities, and evaluation.

Dialogue Journals using **Rallytable**

If two students have read the same book, use one of their journals for a dialogue journal. This technique is also called silent dialogue. In a Rallytable, students pass one journal back and forth across the table like a ping pong ball, writing to each other in turn. Each student assumes the persona of one of the characters in the book and the two write a dialogue or conversation as those characters would. Dialogues that are similar to what the book's characters would say will reflect the writer's skill in using tone, voice, and characterization. In discussing why their dialogues are (or are not) true to the characters in the book, students will discover concepts such as voice and tone. You simply take the opportunity to pin the labels on the concepts.

References:

Graves, Donald H. B*uild a Literate Classroom.* Portsmouth, NH, Heinemann Educational Books, 1991

Murray, Donald M. *Write to Learn.* Fort Worth, Texas, Holt, Rinehard and Winston, Inc., 1990

Weiderhold, Chuck. *The Question Matrix.* San Juan Capistrano, CA, Kagan Cooperative Learning Co., 1991

My thanks to **Dr. Marian Matthews, Dr. Penny Stewart, Nell Jones** and the participants in the 1992 High Plains Writing Project at Eastern New Mexico University for sharing some of the ideas appearing in this section.

Virginia DeBolt: *Write! Cooperative Learning and the Writing Process*
Kagan Cooperative Learning • 1 (800) WEE CO-OP

189

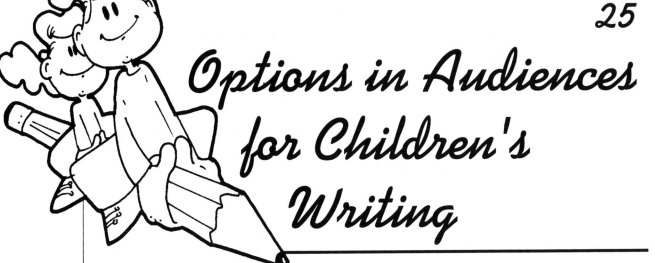

Options in Audiences for Children's Writing

Books. Sturdily bound copies of students' work can be placed in classroom or school library. Books also make good gifts for family members.

Newspapers. Some localities feature schools' and children's work in regular news features. Students can publish their own school newspaper.

Letters. Opportunities for letter writing are as numerous as dandelions in spring.

Bulletin boards, halls, doors. Writing can be posted in rooms and buildings, enticing readers.

Read-Ins. A classroom Read-In every six weeks provides an opportunity for students to share their best work.

Readings. Students go to other classrooms to read their writing aloud.

Assemblies. Ceremonial author's parties or assemblies can be occasions for sharing writing.

Yearbooks. Class compilations about themselves, with pictures, stimulate writing during the year.

Anthologies. Students prepare an anthology of the best work from each student to be bound as a book. Students can also publish anthologies of work by a favorite author (e.g. poems by David McCord) and write the introductory and transitional material themselves.

Public Address. Holidays and other special events offer students an opportunity to share information and ideas over the school's public address system.

Class Magazine. Publish journals to distribute throughout the school. Riddle magazines, historical magazines, cooking magazines, and more.

Time Capsule. Fill a time capsule to be opened at a future date.

Personal. Students enjoy writing to express private or personal ideas in journals or diaries.

Posters. Advertising, slogans, announcements, and other material can be printed on posters.

Performance. Songs, plays, and puppet shows invite performance.

Games. Student research could lead to the creation of games.

Time Lines. Descriptions and pictures of an era under study fill in a time line.

Field Guides. Characteristics of a particular species, illustrated and bound as books.

Recipes. Good for gift giving.

Coloring books. Pictures with accompanying text can be reproduced for sharing with classmates or younger students.

Author's Chair. Allow one or two students to read aloud daily.

Publications That Accept Children's Work

The Acorn. Open to authors in grades K-12. Betty Mowery, Editor. 1530 7th St. Rock Island, IL 61201.

Caboodle: By Kids for Kids. P.O. Box 1049, Portland, IN 47371. Tip sheet available.

Creative Kids. Fay L. & Marvin J. Gold. P.O. Box 6448, 350 Weinacker Ave., Mobile, AL 36660-0448. Guidelines are available.

Cricket, The Magazine for Children. Marianne Carus, Editor-in-Chief. Carus Publishing Co., 315 Fifth Street, Peru, IL 61354.

Merlyn's Pen. P.O. Box 716, East Greenwich, Rhode Island 02818.

Reflections, A National Magazine Publishing Student Writing. Dean Harper, Ed., P.O. Box 368, Duncan Falls, OH 43734. Publishes fiction, nonfiction and poetry twice yearly.

Shoe Tree: The Literary Magazine By and For Children. Joyce McDonald. National Association for Young Writers, P.O. Box 452. Belvidere, NJ 07823. Address also listed is 215 Valle del Sol Drive, Santa Fe, NM 87501. Contests offer prizes.

Stone Soup: The Magazine by Children. Ms. Gerry Mandel, Editor. Children's Art Foundation, P.O. Box 83, Santa Cruz, CA 95063.

The Children's Album. Margo M. Lemas, Editor. EGW Publishing Co., Box 6068 Concord, CA 94524.

Wombat: A Journal of Young People's Writing and Art. 365 Ashton Drive, Athens, GA 30606. Guidelines are available.

Also, consult the current *Writer's Market* published by Writer's Digest Books, Cincinnati, Ohio, and *Market Guide for Young Writers* by Kathy Henderson from Better Way Publications, P.O. Box 219, Crozet, VA 22932.

Virginia DeBolt: *Write! Cooperative Learning and the Writing Process*

192   Kagan Cooperative Learning • 1 (800) WEE CO-OP

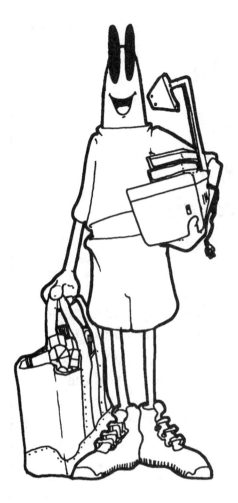

Permission to Appear in

WRITE!
Cooperative Learning and the Writing Process
by Virginia DeBolt

I hereby grant permission for the writing of my child to appear in future editions of the book *Write! Cooperative Learning and the Writing Process.* I understand that this copyrighted work will be sold by Kagan Cooperative Learning, and that my child will receive one copy of the book as sole compensation.

(Please print)

Child's Name_____

Title of Child's Written Work_____

Child's School, City and Grade_____

_____

_____

Child's Home Address _____

_____

Parent's Signature_____

Date_____

Publisher: **Kagan Cooperative Learning, San Juan Capistrano, CA**
Copyright: **Kagan Cooperative Learning**

About the Author

Virginia DeBolt

Virginia DeBolt grew up in Colorado, an only child with her nose stuck in a book. She received a B.A. in English and Elementary Education from Adams State College of Colorado and an M.A. in Elementary Education at the University of Northern Colorado. Since graduating she has enjoyed courses in writing, cooperative learning, photography, astronomy, ceramics, computing, and education.

Virginia was a teacher in Colorado and New Mexico for 26 years. Her teaching experiences include team teaching, nongraded teaching, departmentalized teaching, and self-contained classroom teaching. She has been a Chapter 1 reading specialist, worked in adult education, trained teachers, thrown out the English basal in favor of writing workshop, and come to appreciate cooperative learning as the best of the best.

Virginia has two college-age children, and keeps fit with walking, swimming, and T'ai Chi. She enjoys moviegoing, health and fitness activities, and reading, especially women authors.

While teaching Junior High Virginia began her writing career. In addition to this book, she has written articles, prize winning children's fiction, poetry, short stories, and presently is writing a novel for middle graders.

Virginia DeBolt recently moved to Austin, Texas, where she writes and does educational consulting.

Getting in the Last Word

I love writing and writers. Finding great writing and writers rates very high on my list of favorite pastimes. I get excited when I discover phrases such as, "the day was adangle with shouts and explosions," in what I read, and I pause, adangle myself, to wonder at the mind of Toni Morrison who wrote this delightful word "adangle." I get excited reading the books writers publish about writing. Natalie Goldberg's *Long Quiet Highway*, Annie Dillard's *The Writing Life*, or Lucy McCormick Calkins' *Living Between the Lines*— these women write the music of my heart and soul.

The gurus of writing don't hold exclusive rights to great writing, however. I get excited about kids' writing. Who, but a child, would write that he promises never to slide under the seats on the school bus again "because it isn't sophisticated." Where, but in a classroom filled with young minds, could you hear one boy respond to another's poem called Crusty Panties by declaring it "intellectually stimulating."

Connecting Kagan's Structural Approach to Cooperative Learning with my interest in writing with kids in schools has been a labor of love. My efforts to create a book that teachers will use, will find valuable, will consider a helpful resource were pleasurable work. Spencer Kagan and the people of Kagan Cooperative Learning added painstaking attention to editing, organizing, formating, and illustrating *Write! Cooperative Learning and the Writing Process*, making contributions equal to my own. Celso Rodriguez did the illustrations, Catherine Hurlbert, the graphics and formatting. My thanks to them all.

I hope when you use this book in your classroom you get excited exploring the thoughts, imagery, wonder, and soul songs in children's writing.

References

Calkins, Lucy McCormick with Shelley Harwayne. *Living Between the Lines.* Portsmouth, NH: Heinemann Educational Books, Inc., 1991.

Dillard, Annie. *The Writing Life.* New York, NY: HarperCollins, 1989.

Goldberg, Natalie. *Long Quiet Highway: Waking Up in America.* New York, NY: Bantam Books, 1993.

Morrison, Toni. *Sula.* New York, NY: Alfred A. Knopf, 1973.

Suggestions for Book Binding

A simple, quick and durable book can be made with covers of laminated construction paper. Simply staple it together. Have the student make a cover telling the title, author, and perhaps, with illustration. After the cover is cut in the desired size and shape it can be laminated.

Cardboard covered with cloth, contact paper, wrapping paper, or wallpaper makes a good book cover. Use a hole punch to make several holes for brads, yarn or ribbon for binding the book.

If your class makes a magazine anthology or journal as a culminating activity for the year, consider having it bound with a plastic spiral.